MODERN NOVELISTS

General Editor: Norman Page

MODERN NOVELISTS

MODERN NOVELISTS

D. H. LAWRENCE

G. M. Hyde

St. Martin's Press   New York

First published in the United States of America in 1990

Printed in Hong Kong

ISBN 0–312–04038–5

Library of Congress Cataloging-in-Publication Data
Hyde, G. M. (George M.), 1941–
D.H. Lawrence / G.M. Hyde
    p.   cm. — G.M. Hyde.
Includes bibliographical references.
ISBN 0–312–04038–5
1. Lawrence, D. H. (David Herbert), 1885–1930—Criticism and
interpretation.   I. Title.   II. Series.
PR6023.A93Z631920   1990
823′.912—dc20
                                                89–70032
                                                    CIP

Contents

Acknowledgments

If there are rather few references to other critics in my study, it does not imply disrespect, or that my own book does not owe a great deal to the immense body of work on Lawrence. I would like to record a special debt to those involved in the new Cambridge edition; and to Colin Clarke, who took the trouble to read the manuscript with his usual generosity, care and critical acumen.

General Editor's Preface

The death of the novel has often been announced, and part of the secret of its obstinate vitality must be its capacity for growth, adaptation, self-renewal and even self-transformation: like some vigorous organism in a speeded-up Darwinian ecosystem, it adapts itself quickly to a changing world. War and revolution, economic crisis and social change, radically new ideologies such as Marxism and Freudianism, have made this century unprecedented in human history in the speed and extent of change, but the novel has shown an extraordinary capacity to find new forms and techniques and to accommodate new ideas and conceptions of human nature and human experience, and even to take up new positions on the nature of fiction itself.

In the generations immediately preceding and following 1914, the novel underwent a radical redefinition of its nature and possibilities. The present series of monographs is devoted to the novelists who created the modern novel and to those who, in their turn, either continued and extended, or reacted against and rejected, the traditions established during that period of intense exploration and experiment. It includes a number of those who lived and wrote in the nineteenth century but whose innovative contribution to the art of fiction makes it impossible to ignore them in any account of the origins of the modern novel; it also includes the so-called 'modernists' and those who in the mid and later twentieth century have emerged as outstanding practitioners in this genre. The scope is, inevitably, international; not only, in the migratory and exile-haunted world of our century, do writers refuse to heed national frontiers – 'English' literature lays claims to Conrad the Pole, Henry James the American, and Joyce the Irishman – but geniuses such as Flaubert, Dostoevsky and Kafka have had an influence on the fiction of many nations.

Each volume in the series is intended to provide an introduction to the fiction of the writer concerned, both for those approaching him or her for the first time and for those who are already familiar with some parts of the achievement in question and now wish to place it in the context of the total *oeuvre*. Although essential information relating to the writer's life and times is given, usually in an opening chapter, the approach is primarily critical and the emphasis is not upon 'background' or generalisations but upon close examination of important texts. Where an author is notably prolific, major texts have been selected for detailed attention but an attempt has also been made to convey, more summarily, a sense of the nature and quality of the author's work as a whole. Those who want to read further will find suggestions in the select bibliography included in each volume. Many novelists are, of course, not only novelists but also poets, essayists, biographers, dramatists, travel writers and so forth; many have practised shorter forms of fiction; and many have written letters or kept diaries that constitute a significant part of their literary output. A brief study cannot hope to deal with all these in detail, but where the shorter fiction and the non-fictional writings, public and private, have an important relationship to the novels, some space has been devoted to them.

NORMAN PAGE

For Barbara, Matthew and Edward

Introduction

D. H. Lawrence belonged to a generation of writers who were still in touch with a kind of moral and artistic heroism that is hard to recuperate in a consumer culture. In some ways closer to the nineteenth century than to the twentieth (like his self-appointed acolyte F. R. Leavis),[1] Lawrence carried forward into our own time the aura of the unique individual experience as the touchstone of authenticity in all things, political, social and personal. One of the Last Romantics, and imbued with the spirit of the great Victorian prophets, Lawrence nevertheless encountered the modern world not just in the form of Arnold's 'strange disease of modern life', but in more specifically corrosive guises: a War, for instance, in which he was involved by marriage almost as painfully as if he had fought in it; that other continuing war between the sexes which the sheer monumentality of Victorian patriarchy had suppressed; the breakup of nineteenth-century nation states in an atmosphere of political violence (impinging directly on Lawrence's Lost Generation version of the Grand Tour); Modernism in painting and sculpture as well as in literature, which shattered the tenuous nineteenth-century consensus about 'realism' and 'the old stable ego'; and perhaps at the root of all this the crisis of faith, which in Lawrence takes the form of a painful resurrection of the body from under the heavy moral tombstone of Victorian agnosticism and the Puritan burden of guilt and shame.

Lawrence's heroism is, like Baudelaire's 'héroisme de la vie moderne',[2] an art of contradictions, paradoxes, and (above all) survival. The 'chameleon poet' (Keats's term) refuses – like the moral order of the novel, according to Lawrence – to be 'nailed down'.[3] Lawrence has often been misinterpreted by admirers as well as detractors who fail to see that his world is in *process*. The rainbow, as Wordsworth succinctly observed, comes and goes, and Lawrence invested a religious trust in the wind that bloweth where it listeth. This existential openness does not always combine happily with his innate didacticism. Nor, inevitably, did it bring the normal rewards (and challenges) of a successful career and settled

1

family life, so that we find a strident note in the work of the 'middle period' (mid and late twenties) and a continuing marital struggle that may have been inevitable, given the degree of faith he invested in that single 'pure' relationship. In the circumstances, it is remarkable that Lawrence's vision survived so powerfully in *Lady Chatterley's Lover*, which changed the institutional culture before being absorbed by it. But it is equally clear that Lawrence's development was distorted by the fact that he was so much of a loner by temperament and choice as well as by necessity.

Despite everything, Lawrence remains a cultural force to be reckoned with: one of those writers about whom (as Eliot says of Shakespeare) we evidently have to keep changing our ways of being wrong. For my generation, he was a particular sort of culture hero. The grammar-school boy made good had turned into the radical individualist challenging the 'machinery' of our civilisation and crusading against tawdry 'American' values. He could also, when common sense demanded, put down the over-refined spokespersons of 'high' culture (who had lost touch with 'Life'); especially, it sometimes seemed, the female of the species. Lawrence, aided by F. R. Leavis, rose to this extraordinary eminence only after his death. In his lifetime he was largely without honour, and this fact lent weight to Leavis's 'mass civilisation, minority culture' reading of his life and works. In the 1930s, he was anathematised as a crypto-Fascist by right-thinking left-wingers who disliked his 'belief in the blood as wiser than the intellect'.[4] Another metamorphosis many will recall is Lawrence the Hippy, preaching love on the road (so to speak) and 'into' various ways of Doing Your Own Thing (many of which shared a common ancestry with Lawrence's Puritanism, and had come home with a new urgency from a society steeped in consumerism and fighting an unjust war). The Lawrence of the 1960s and early 1970s was a flat-earthing organicist relating on 'I – Thou' terms with everything/body from a Bat or a Gentian to his friends and would-be lovers. In this way, one powerful component of Lawrence's imaginative world was inflated to fill the whole. This man of straw seemed to many to have been finally discredited by Feminist theory which, following Kate Millett's tendentious reading,[5] discovered in Lawrence's 'love ethic' a systematic belittling, manipulation, and domination of women, and dismissed his battle with the censors as a covert justification of pornography. More recently some women commentators have redrawn the boundaries between the pornographic and the erotic, and some have credited Lawrence with trying to see the world through a woman's eyes,[6] even if he could not begin to understand what the Women's Movement was about, and clung to his faith in marriage to the bitter end.

And if we address ourselves to the central enigma of this writer who has counted so enormously in forming the dissident, or critical, ideology of English in our time (and remains a potent influence), we may locate it in a paradox of Nietzsche: 'what we have words for, we have already got beyond.' Lawrence writes as if feeling, thinking, and writing were one and indivisible; and as if literature, by means of what he liked to call 'art speech', were indeed the Word Made Flesh. Knowing, at the same time, that this cannot be the case, he engages in the Modernist struggle to resurrect the word through 'transcodings', subverting and extending the bounds of possibility. The recent publication of *Mr Noon* has shown how he might have opened up another vein in his enormous imaginative resources (one already suggested by *The Lost Girl*) and dealt more comprehensively with the English society he came back to belatedly, in romance guise, in *Lady Chatterley's Lover*.

Lawrence's works, especially his novels, continue to generate dialogue, because however extreme or provoking the positions he may take up, he never suggests that the last word has been said. Ken Russell's film of *Women in Love*, a highly visual, even cinematic novel, came close to engaging Lawrence in a definitive modern dialogue. Other films, like the recent *Lady Chatterley's Lover*, *The Virgin and the Gypsy*, and *The Fox*, while more commercial, have nevertheless responded to Lawrence's vivid sense of place and space. Students, I find, still want to engage Lawrence in dialogues, about sex, religion, nature, and writing. This impulse can coexist with considerable impatience or hostility. My own study is the work of an unrepentant admirer trying to register cogent reasons for reading Lawrence now. I begin with a kind of 'overture', in the shape of a chapter tracing the themes of Lawrence's life and works. The reader will find that these themes expand, like Proust's Japanese flowers, in the course of the book.

1
Life and Works

David Herbert Lawrence (to restore to him the first names he disliked and rarely used) was born in border country, in a part of Nottinghamshire that is next to Derbyshire, on 11 September 1885. The idea of being 'in between' figured largely in Lawrence's own habitual myth-making[1] alongside his peculiarly intense awareness of identity, so that even in introducing basic factual information we are made conscious of the symbolic properties of family and place and of the play of differences that organises all his work. The border between Nottinghamshire and Derbyshire may not be marked by outstanding geographical features, yet it codes, for Lawrence, deeper, more subjective boundaries between mother and father, father and son, mother and son: the disputed territory in which sons are also lovers (and haters). When he came to maturity, Lawrence travelled far and wide, advocating a life lived 'fully on the spot where you are': but his pilgrimages remain in touch with the psychic geography of his childhood and adolescence. Moreover, eternally in process as he was, forever 'becoming', Lawrence was abnormally aware of other selves left behind or 'transcended', places that have lost their magic and become 'no good', as well as promised lands waiting to be named. In this interplay of roles and identities, in the ritualised and sometimes theatrical construction of a 'site' where the drama may be fittingly played out, we find a kind of eternal return of material from childhood: and although Lawrence never, strictly speaking, 'went back', the real and imaginary landscapes of his early days stayed with him.

The mythologies of class and family that Lawrence later elaborated into his acerbic and influential 'sociology' of English culture originated with the tensions between his coal-miner father and genteel mother in the close, but by no means benighted, working-class community of Eastwood. The story has often been told (by

4

Ada Lawrence Clarke, for example, and in more detail by Harry T. Moore in his standard biography) of how the dashing collier, Arthur Lawrence, met the serious and refined ex-schoolteacher, Lydia Beardsall, while visiting Nottingham from Brinsley, and captivated her with a charm which gradually wore thin and gave way to open animosity on both sides. Lydia's fourth child (and her third son) was the novelist, and he seems indeed to have been as precariously situated on the frontiers of life and death as *Sons and Lovers* tells us. Working upon, and through, the Christian symbolism which he absorbed from his Congregationalist upbringing, Lawrence began from an early age to write his own 'myth of the birth of the hero'[2] and his highly coloured fictional interpretation of his life was not distinct, either now or later on, from life as it was lived. The birth of Paul Morel (the fictionalised Lawrence of *Sons and Lovers* is marked by portents and a sharp sundering of the father and the mother, so that Mrs Morel is impregnated as it were by the Holy Ghost, and Paul's birth (and his subsequent baptism in blood) are mystic events.[3] The dead William[4] is by this means relegated to the status of a forerunner. The women in Paul's life are even more strikingly cast in auxiliary and quasi-scriptural roles as madonnas and Mary Magdalenes. Writing is inextricably bound up with scripture, in the sense that the stirring of Lawrence's artistic sensibility is soon mythologised as a kind of Pilgrim's Progress towards salvation, and through personal salvation the redemption of a suffering, divided humanity. Lawrence saw himself as a casualty of the modern age, the Age of Love (or Spirit), the New Testament era of abstraction and the industrialism that went hand in hand with the triumph of the free individual consciousness. The Son, born of love, is crucified on the contradiction between freedom and necessity. Necessity is embodied in Old Testament Law, the power and irrationality of the Father. Writing, if it is inspired (breathed into by the Spirit) can act as reconciler, the Holy Ghost that intervenes between the bound and the free, the individual and the organic bonds of the group, the spoken and unspoken worlds.

This Puritan intensity, the ceaseless quest for a symbolic order behind events and experiences which most of us accept and reject on their own terms, is implicated in every facet of Lawrence's life and work, not least in the fraught and complex relationship with the girl called Miriam in *Sons and Lovers*, in real life Jessie

Chambers, daughter of a local farmer. Lawrence met her in 1901
and their relationship had still by no means resolved itself when he
left England with Frieda Weekley in 1912 (when *Sons and Lovers*
was still being revised). Jessie was 'different' from the girlfriend
that Ernest (the William of *Sons and Lovers*) had brought home
from London, Gypsy Dennis (the Louisa Lily Denys Western of
Sons and Lovers). Jessie's sensitivity and reserve complemented her
dark good looks to form, in the young Lawrence's Victorian view, a
fitting soul mate. But it was just these qualities that confirmed in
Jessie the image of, and rivalry with, his mother, and led to
Lawrence's self-defeating projection on to her of his sexual anxieties. In one of its more clear-sighted comments on the relationship, *Sons and Lovers* speaks (half through Paul's consciousness)
of Miriam as the 'threshing-floor' on which the young artist
thrashed out his ideas. A displaced and forbidden sexuality
charged their relationship (on his part, mainly) with a gloomy
intensity precisely in that domain of shared interests (literature, the
arts, music) where the 'mother in the mind' intervened. Jessie
interpreted their discussions of (for instance) French poetry as
complex and abstract expressions of sexual desire: but Paul presents his versions of Baudelaire as frustrated attempts on his part
to initiate her: not quite the same thing. In general, the protagonist
of the novel seems not to recognise (any more than the author did)
that he is using, or abusing, a 'cultural' power in an attempt to tame
a 'natural' force (female sexuality). Jessie's *Personal Record*[5] does
something to redress the balance, but she was too deeply wounded
by the young Lawrence's overbearing impotence to be objective.
Ironically, it was with her help that his work first appeared in
print.[6]

By the time *Sons and Lovers* was published (1913), the intense
courtship of Lawrence and Jessie had undergone many (mainly
painful) transformations: largely, in Jessie's view, in response to
Lawrence's more and more articulate rejection of the sexual
inhibitions of late Victorianism and the distortions of sexuality
which it generated. Frieda played a major part here: the sexually
liberated Prussian aristocrat, wife of Lawrence's professor of
German in Nottingham, she offered a marked contrast to Jessie's
reserve, shocking and intriguing Lawrence by her forwardness.
She also offered him a partial but lasting release from the sexual
block generated by the closeness of his relationship with his

mother, the Oedipus complex.[7] For the young artist in revolt against authority in all its manifestations (and the power of the Father in particular) there was an ecstatic liberation, recorded in fact and fantasy in (especially) the poetry of the period as well as in *The Rainbow*, in the successful intervention of the Son between Father and Mother. The affair that Paul has with Clara in *Sons and Lovers* (referring to a specific real-life episode)[8] also involves the intrusion of the protagonist into the 'closed' marital relationship, with (in this case) a strongly defined symbolic assault on the Father (Clara's husband Baxter); but Clara's prototype was actually quite matter of fact about her transgression of wedlock. Lawrence needed the confirmation of his potency to be offered by the *otherness* of his sexual partner, and this Frieda (alien, aristocratic, and incorporated into the systems of 'high' culture which he and Jessie and his mother had only scratched the surface of) was uniquely qualified to offer. *Mr Noon* gives a vivid account of the courtship, with a strong emphasis on the sexual chanciness that continued to fascinate Lawrence in Frieda. Tom's courtship of Lydia in *The Rainbow* borrows and transposes some of its elements, but mythologising Lydia's forlornness under the guise of Lawrence's favourite Sleeping Beauty story (cf. *Lady Chatterley's Lover*.[9]) The elopement of the two lovers took Lawrence literally to an 'alien' domain, his bride's sinister and enchanted Europe whose magic tongues he commanded. This flight also confirmed the 'difference', the 'inbetweenness' fostered by mother love, so that Lawrence in a sense never made his way back to any 'real' society (the power of his alienated vision lies at the root of his social prophecies, linking him with Blake and Bunyan as well as with Carlyle and Ruskin). In the passionate world of Germany and Italy, with its martyred Christs [10] and violence close to the surface of daily life, the Son could hope to win his battle and realise his dream of supplanting the Father.[11] 'Look, we have come through!' is his joyful cry of release.

When Lawrence met Frieda, he was a tired and sick schoolmaster in Croydon, author of some poems and short stories and of two novels, with a third shortly to be published. Trained as a teacher, first at Ilkeston pupil teacher centre, then at Nottingham University College, Lawrence had ample opportunity not only to add to the store of reading begun by his mother and continued by Jessie but also to experience for himself the tyrannous harshness of middle-

class culture as it forced each sentient being into articulate consciousness. Lawrence experienced as a teacher the consequences of
the 1902 Education Act. Following on from the work of the 1870
Act, this drive to extend the educational franchise seemed to
Lawrence to be doing as much harm as good, as it tried to cope with
the spiritual and emotional deficiencies and damage which indus-
trialisation, and education itself (with its concomitant philosophy of
social climbing and individual success) was causing.[12] His second
novel, *The Trespasser* (1912), is imbued with the spirit of Wagner,
not just as a tribute to a fashionable composer, but in a quest for the
communal tragic spirit which the secular art of the nineteenth
century had exiled but which Wagner and Nietzsche strove to
resuscitate. A Nietzschean dualism runs through Lawrence's art.
The writer strives for form (his medium of expression) but the
writing lays claim to a territory beyond the boundaries of the known
world (and thus beyond the writer's intentions). It is quite proper
to refer, in the modern way, to Lawrence's 'texts', since they live a
life of their own distinct from what the writer may have intended to
'say' by writing them: as Lawrence neatly put it, 'never trust the
artist, trust the tale'.[13]

Rising from the dead is once again the appropriate image: after
his illness of 1912, the schoolmaster took wing, erratically, to fly
(like Joyce) over the nets cast to trap him and hold him back. But it
was the eve of war. Stephen Dedalus has returned to Ireland, at the
beginning of *Ulysses*, because of his mother's death. Lawrence had
lived through his mother's slow death in 1910, but his escape, too,
was short lived. An alien in Frieda's Prussia, Lawrence moved on
with her to Italy, and began work on his masterpiece (published
eventually as two novels, *The Rainbow* and *Women in Love*). But by
mid-1914 they were back in England, in close contact with the
literary circles in which Lawrence had begun to make his way as
early as 1909 when Ford's enterprising *English Review* had published his first pieces. John Middleton Murry and his lover,
Katherine Mansfield, draw particularly close to the Lawrences, and
as the shadows of war closed in, their quadrilateral relationship
grew deeper and more agonising. Much of the agony (as well as the
joy) of it has gone into *Women in Love*, in the intricate geometry of
Birkin and Ursula's relationship with Gerald and Gudrun. The
beginning of the war with Germany in the summer of 1914 had cut
short what had been for Lawrence an expansive period in which he

was beginning to find pleasure in his modest but growing fame (even if he was still very troubled by material worries). Travel to Europe became very difficult, but far worse was the fact that Lawrence, unwelcome as an Englishman in Germany, was now under suspicion in his own country for having recently married a member of a distinguished Prussian military family (Frieda was a von Richthofen). Thoughts of a Utopian community free from war talk, where like-minded individuals could share their lives and their thoughts, came to preoccupy Lawrence, whose 'in-betweenness' was proving burdensome in various ways. Lady Ottoline Morrell's home, Garsington Manor, where she played the part of patroness to an impressive circle of writers and thinkers, offered one possible location. Growing for a time close to Bertrand Russell, with whom he planned to write a series of pacifist lectures, Lawrence was introduced to Cambridge society in 1915, but cordially disliked it. He turned the full force of his 'apocalyptic' vision in *Women In Love* upon what he saw as the personal and political betrayals and failures of understanding of the early years of the War, the violence of which he internalised, as he said, in the characters, instead of locating it in the battlefield. For one thing, the profound connection between rampant capitalism in 'genteel' culture, and the violent oppression of man by man (and woman too) lay at home, not at the front, and Gerald's mines and his death wish expressed them with intricate precision: His terminal 'I didn't want it, really', echoed in Birkin's 'I didn't want it to be like this', is the Kaiser's shocked 'Ich habe es nicht gewollt'. And in the Autumn of 1915 *The Rainbow* was published.

To this day, the intensity of the hostility to this novel has not been adequately explained. The police confiscated it, there was a trial, and the entire edition was burned: ostensibly on the grounds of obscenity. Harry T. Moore has, however, adduced evidence that political reasons weighed equally with the moral arguments, though they could not be made explicit at the time. At all events, there were very few to defend what is now one of the classics of twentieth-century fiction, and it may be more fruitful to explore the reasons why the novel failed to achieve its true status than to go back over what nowadays seem irrelevant objections to its 'obscenity' or tenuous fears as to its subversiveness. *The Rainbow* is Lawrence's search for lost time, begun on the eve of the unprecedented cataclysm that threatened the very foundations of Euro-

pean civilisation: its great cyclical movements of history and myth
feel their way back through Victorianism, exploring the iconography of 'the eunuch century' in an endeavour to identify those
changes in sensibility that increasingly threatened (in the name of
progress and freedom) the ties of community that validated a
'rooted' way of life. The movement, however, does not run simply
against the grain of historical change: like a Yeatsian gyre, a
contrary movement unfolds dialectically within and against the
'widening circle' (*two* chapters bear this title) of loosening 'organic'
ties: this is the historical growth of the idea of selfhood, the free
and autonomous individual, a freedom located above all in the
rising consciousness of women against the oppression of patriarchal myths. Much of Frieda's experience has gone directly into the
novel, but Lawrence also makes use (it may be argued how
legitimately) of the life histories of other women he knew, like
Jessie, Louie Burrows (to whom he was briefly engaged to be
married), Helen Corke, and the 'emancipated' women of the Alice
Dax circle.

The school experiences are partly Louie's and Jessie's, partly
Lawrence's own. Education is a dominant theme because Lawrence
rightly locates in this area the formation of models of consciousness
which dominate contemporary ideology (and are taken for granted
in all 'developed' societies). It need not have been so: Lawrence
scrutinises the iconography of high Victorianism in order to
explore the ways in which concepts of identity were formed and
disseminated in response to a waning faith; Ursula's breakdown at
the end of the novel reproduces a crisis in the value-system of her
age.

The Rainbow is Lawrence's Old Testament, or at least a Genesis
and Exodus, shaped by his Congregationalist upbringing and
written (like *Sons and Lovers*) with a strong sense of spiritual
autobiography (Bunyan's *Pilgrim's Progress* and *Grace Abounding*
invest the moral landscape of the novel with a visionary sense of
value). The ultimate manifestation of the rainbow in the novel is
different in kind from its earlier manifestations: it is apocalyptic
and subjective rather than 'iconic'.[14] Its meanings are constructed
not in relation to scriptural authority but in response to Ursula's
deep personal needs, her *own* sense of crisis which she has to
articulate and (hopefully) share. In *Women in Love*, where the
characters are what Frank Kermode calls 'apocalyptic types',[15] a

fractured, imagistic narrative takes the place of the great cyclical reiterations of *The Rainbow*. Lawrence is responding immediately (as he always did) to his new milieu: indeed, we can already see in *Women in Love* the improvisatory collages and theatrical scenarios of the subsequent pseudo-travelogue fiction.

After the suppression of *The Rainbow* there was an agony of waiting to find a publisher for *Women in Love*, agony compounded by the War and by Lawrence's victimisation and harassment by a state security apparatus which he rightly saw as becoming more and more authoritarian, not to say vindictive. But there was also the intricate and provocative cultural milieu of London's bohemia, Lady Ottoline Morrell's Garsington group, Bloomsbury, and Cambridge. Lawrence thrusts himself abruptly, awkwardly into the midst of this shifting, pluralistic, 'enlightened' world of cultural fragments and pregnant allusions, a world not unlike that of Eliot's 'Waste Land', another bursting and scattering of the great overripe fruit of European culture. Lawrence's nervous self-consciousness as well as his edgy, rasping Protestantism are reproduced in Birkin's self-dramatising rebelliousness, his shaky but tenacious hold on a swirling multiplicity of relationships and personae, cultural and political. In places, *Women in Love* comes close to being a great satirical novel, as diagrammatic sketches and caricatures, often of recognisable, even eminent, personages, rampage through violent and self-destructive charades: Lawrence narrowly avoided being sued by some of his victims. But ultimately *Women in Love* is centred elsewhere (if it can be said to have a 'centre' at all). Lawrence's profoundly visual imagination[16] has led him in this novel away from 'the spoken world'. The troubled friendship of Birkin, Ursula, Gerald, and Gudrun (corresponding in many ways, as I have said, to the Lawrences' friendship with Middleton Murry and Katherine Mansfield) is a kind of vortex of symbolic energy which can be realised, concretised, through the configurations of objects and people who get caught up and 'radiate' in its field of force. Not for nothing does Lawrence involve Italian Futurism when he is trying to explain to Garnett about the troublesome originality of his vision and method.[17] *Women in Love* is an imaginary museum of energised images, heterogeneous and 'exotic', though even the most remote, the 'primitive' carvings and the Chinese goose, are made to function as correlatives of a tension of a very immediate kind in characters themselves.

Women in Love was completed in 1916, but Lawrence could not find a publisher for it until Thomas Selzer brought out a subscription edition in New York in 1920. The stresses of 1915/16, the Lawrences' 'nightmare year', the poverty and isolation of their life in Cornwall with Murry and Katherine, the harrassment to which they were subjected by the Home Office and the police, embittered Lawrence for ever. Yet out of his agonised friendship with Murry he made the great prophetic dialectic of Birkin and Gerald's love; even the search for second-hand furniture for Murry's cottage becomes a resonant symbolic crux in Lawrence's novel. The nightmare year figures again in *Kangaroo*, with the hero looking back in anger on the humiliations of those times: yet with Lawrence negation and creativity always go hand in hand. Towards the end of the War, Lawrence felt once again his urge to found a Utopian community, his 'Rananim'.[18] His image of this unrealisable society owes much to Morris-style socialism, and before that to the 'pantisocracies' and other earthly paradises of English Romanticism. America was to be the place where the new community could flourish: yet characteristically he was to reach the New World only via the old, for when the end of the War made travel once again possible, he set off for Italy, where Frieda was to join him.

In these early post-war years, with *Women in Love* still unpublished, Lawrence's work underwent a profound (if not altogether enduring) change. The problem of marketing his work was immediate, and letters of the period reflect his straitened financial circumstances. The end of the War was for Lawrence a watershed in European culture: consciousness had again changed irreversibly, but in ways that the elaborate modernist narrative of *Women in Love* could not reach. Two novels, *The Lost Girl* (begun before the War, but substantially rewritten after it, and published in 1920) and *Mr Noon* (left incomplete in 1921, published in full only in 1984) are surprising on first encounter by virtue of the fact that they return to a small provincial world. On one level, the motivation for this is clear enough: Lawrence felt that he could beat Arnold Bennett on his home ground, and be at least as successful a chronicler of Midlands life as Bennett had been. But the letters of the period reveal a different, and subtler, ambition. Lawrence actively disliked what he saw as Bennett's cold 'Frenchified' approach to provincial England, and the famous 'form' that (it was claimed) Bennett's work displayed and Lawrence's lacked seemed to the latter cramping and constricting.[19] As responses to Bennett, *The Lost Girl* and *Mr Noon* both engage with the question of what 'popular' fiction might look like if it were not written to a formula derived from the melodramatic naturalism of Maupassant, and could escape from the constraints of Victorianism. Lawrence in some ways picks up from Dickens, especially *Hard Times*, in his creation of a fantasy world of play-acting in *The Lost Girl* as an antidote to the gritty sobriety of Woodhouse; and in this novel as in *Mr Noon*, the playful, self-conscious, 'folksy' narrative voice invokes a world of music-hall patter, story-telling and charade posited upon a quite different set of relations with the reader than we find in Lawrence's earlier fiction. Digressive, intimate, heterogeneous, and sometimes strangely candid, these two novels catch a transient mood of gaiety and optimism in Lawrence, a post-war hopefulness that also has its darker side. When Alvina (like Lawrence) comes to rest in the Italian mountains, there are ominous undertones of war: it is doubtful if Ciccio will return. *The Lost Girl* ends on a note of insecurity and uncertainty, and *Mr Noon*'s gaiety ends with a question mark. This was Lawrence's characteristic way of 'ending' (every end being a beginning elsewhere); but this time it meant the start of a decade of self-imposed exile.

The writing came faster than ever, and had about it a raw, improvised, cobbled-together look. *Aaron's Rod*, begun in 1918, was published in 1922, and its first paragraph sets the tone of the times: 'The war was over, and there was a sense of relief that was almost a new menace.' It chronicles Aaron's flight from the provincial domesticity evoked in Bennett's work, and handled with nice irreverence in *The Lost Girl* and *Mr Noon*. Breaking the Mosaic tablets of the Law, Aaron chooses the 'irresponsibility' of self-sufficiency: the chapter in which he eavesdrops on his own family, done in that estranged manner of which David Storey (Lawrence's contemporary successor) is the present-day master, chillingly suggests the author's plunge into abstraction, his complete break with the sinking coffin of England. Pages of dialogue with little authorial comment, apparently transcribed more or less from life, mask (they do not articulate) deep feelings, which explode inconclusively in physical action: a punch, a quasi-homosexual caress, an anarchist's bomb. The violence of *Women in Love*, which Lawrence specifically correlated with the War but dealt with on the personal level, has passed beyond personal relations, flowing into inarticulate political outbursts against (for instance) marriage as an institution. No longer is there a containment and exorcism of the death wish (as in Birkin and Ursula's struggle for wholeness); nor is there a privileged domain of subjectivity. Lawrence's raw exposure, the unresolved tensions between himself and Frieda, are barely fictionalised: 'Thoughts something in this manner ran through Aaron's subconscious mind as he sat in the strange house. He could not have fired it all off at any listener, as these pages are fired off at any chance reader.' With subjectivity made public in this way, Lawrence's mind comes back more and more often to reflections upon power, though without leaving behind altogether love and the polarised equilibrium he had sought so earnestly.

Still, these post-war years in Italy are not, as I have said, altogether summed up by the accelerating political and sexual strife of *Aaron's Rod*, and even in this novel there is much sharp and sardonic humour. Breaking with Murry and Katherine (and shamefully vituperative to both of them), Lawrence befriended the strange figure of Maurice Magnus, a cosmopolitan drifter who had attached himself to Norman Douglas. Lawrence used him as the prototype of Mr May in *The Lost Girl* (guying his enthusiasm for his 'erection', the playhouse) yet the relationship, in which Magnus sponged off Lawrence, and Lawrence tried to straighten out Magnus's confused personal affairs, went deeper than this caricature suggests. Lawrence supplied a fine introduction for Magnus's *Memoirs of the Foreign Legion*, published in 1924 after Magnus, at the end of his tether, had poisoned himself. Magnus was a 'good rat, *determined* not to be trapped': to the Lawrence of *The Lost Girl* and *Aaron's Rod* he represented a lonely (if grotesque) human pride. He had style, and 'he carried the human consciousness through circumstances which would have been too much for me'. The two men were not really close, but Lawrence doubtless saw something of himself in Magnus (and not just of the 'there but for the grace of God' kind) and seemed to take pride in being able to do justice to a man who was (in the eyes of the world) just human flotsam. Through Magnus, Lawrence felt he could embrace the 'foul rotten spirit of mankind' and strengthen resistance to 'the monstrous machines of war'. *Inter alia* Lawrence gives utterance in this Introduction to what we might properly call a Dostoevskyan world-view: in this unforeseen way his extensive study of Dostoevsky, undertaken with and against Murry, bore fruit.

Moreover, the growing mysogyny of Lawrence's writing in this period is tempered by another set of feelings, emerging at their most positive as a kind of jokey comradeship with Frieda. *Sea and Sardinia* (1921) is in this respect an effective counterweight to *Aaron's Rod*, and Lawrence seems to have felt that whatever the difficulties of his marriage, the partnership was altogether preferable to the empty promiscuities of the smart expatriate set of Capri and other choice Italian refuges. This volume of travel sketches gains much of its extraordinary vividness from the interaction, sometimes dramatised, sometimes merely stated, between 'the queen bee' (or just 'Q.B.' for short), Frieda, and her long-suffering husband. In *Fantasia of the Unconscious* (1922), *Studies in Classic American Literature* (1923), and the poems and novellas of the period, Lawrence is in full command of his powers, and still (in perhaps a more abstract way than before) committed to charting the stormy waters of sexual relations. He was also becoming a skilful translator, working his way through some of the major writings of the Sicilian, Giovanni Verga.[20] Translation was for Lawrence another border country in which he could explore relationships, in this case between the living bodies (in Verga's word the '*fisonomia*') of two languages. Much of the fascination of Lawrence's translations of Verga lies in his predilection for tracing with his English the contours of Verga's 'Sicialianate' Italian, taking something like an erotic pleasure in fitting his Nottingham dialect around the quick and sensitive Italian idioms.

Yet another mother figure was about to enter Lawrence's life, and she at once set up a rivalry with the Queen Bee. This was Mabel Dodge Luhan, an American patroness more formidable in her way than Lady Ottoline had been. Mabel Dodge Luhan (or Mabel Sterne as she then still was) called out to Lawrence's Utopianism, the dream that still haunted him of 'starting again' (but this time on a more modest scale, with a farm of manageable proportions). The Lawrences characteristically sailed East to reach the West, visiting Ceylon and stopping off in Australia, and here Lawrence completed *Kangaroo* (1923) in the space of six weeks before following the call of the American frontier (the glamour of which he had himself marvellously evoked in *Studies in Classic American Literature* a year or two earlier). Something of the spirit of Maurice Magnus has entered *Kangaroo*: even more than *Aaron's Rod* it is improvised, unrevised, opportunist in the best sense, and its Lawrencian protagonist, while still deeply imbued with Lawrence's Puritanism, has Magnus's gift of embracing negation, transience, the emptiness at the heart of the human world. Australia inspired Lawrence for much the same perverse reason that it seems to have inspired Australian writers: an elemental simplicity in the inhuman landscape coexists with the worst debris of European 'conveniences' (as Lawrence scornfully called them). There are, as Patrick White has said, very few distractions. It was a good place to study the way that the War had killed the spiritual quick of Europe, and to trace the unseen forces engendering the future.

Lawrence's scenario (and I use this word advisedly) projects the struggle between fascist and anarchist forces that he had lived through in Italy, writ large in the absence of European constraints. The fear and dislike of emergent fascism (as in *Sea and Sardinia*, for instance) gives way, in *Kangaroo*, to a fascination with power struggles, and with power itself. Lawrence begins to see how the collapse of Law in the era of Love[21] and the failure of the religious creeds sanctifying the family as the repository of spiritual truth and human values[22] inevitably transposes the power struggle 'out there' in the political world on to the married relations of men and women. The Puritan culture which Lawrence grew up within, with its tendency to idealise women as well as its magnanimously patriarchal recognition of their notional equality, had already run up against Lawrence's first-hand experience of the realistic Italian view of sex as a power game: but in Italy the rules of the game were known. In Australia Lawrence seems to have experienced a kind of sexual anarchy, a moral disorientation of his marriage to which he responded with assertions of 'phallic' power. Thus although Somers feels 'the vacancy of freedom' as a threat, he is also fascinated at the same time by the possibilities it offers for being one's own man.

The years of exile were telling: the uprootedness and the (maybe self-imposed) failure to 'count' in the world, even in the world of letters, had begun to generate in Lawrence a restless desire for some sort of power: a power which he inevitably confused with his Utopian, Puritan faith in a new social order. Great tracts of political debate, arid as the Australian bush yet sometimes (as in *Kangaroo*'s anecdote of the ant-hill) breaking into lurid bloom, thrown almost arbitrarily together and interspersed with travelogue, press-cuttings – these are all, in Lawrence's own word, 'bits', the fragments of a shattered and irrecoverable totality, the debris of European materialism piled up round the neat bungalows in depressing heaps. The 'Nightmare' chapter is (like 'Harriet and Lovat at sea in marriage') a set piece, in this case harking back to the humiliations of 1916 and the repeated searchings and strippings and accusations. Yet it does not seem out of place in the context of Lovat Somers' Australian political debates, since 1916 marked, for Lawrence, the end of 'the old world' in more senses than one. The 'bittiness' of the Australian popular press is reflected in Somers' own tense and self-contradictory state of mind, and Lawrence's almost unmediated, 'immediate' response to an unformed continent searching for an image of itself.

The Lawrences arrived in and left Australia in the space of a few months, trekking on towards the disillusioning frontier of Taos and Mabel Sterne, its *genius loci*. Inevitably, being under the tutelage of a rich patroness aroused the kinds of stresses and resentments that Lawrence had already worked through in *Women in Love*, *vis-à-vis* Lady Ottoline Morrell; but his response to the New World was nevertheless characteristically vivid. He revives ancient myths and weaves new ones around them, but simultaneously pushes away the stock responses of exotic travelogue, clearing new ground like the assiduous pioneer that he was. In the life of the Indians Lawrence found 'the pure wonder of creation': not the Judaeo-Hellenic world of the supreme creator and man his creature, but cycles of creation from the void. *Mornings in Mexico* (1927) opens with a chapter about a dog and a parrot that makes fun of him: a tense 'antediluvian' conflict across the 'gulf of the other dimension' captures the non-human abrasiveness of Mexico. In *The Plumed Serpent* (finished by 1924) Lawrence had dramatised the revival of the old gods in a parable strangely reminiscent of the apocalyptic Christianity of his youth.[23] Its middle-aged protagonist, Kate Lesley, is 'initiated' into a religion of male power that takes the form of a revolutionary political movement. In *Mornings in Mexico* the striving and the stridency are subdued to the defamiliarising and sceptical vision. Both books share, however, the improvisatory style of much of Lawrence's later writing. The 'author' is relinquishing, however reluctantly, the final control of his created world, often content merely to cite and transcribe and be lost in the drama. *The Plumed Serpent*, like the short stories of this period, is theatrical in more senses than one. Melodramatic and even lurid, these works simultaneously invoke and negate the God-like power of the writer. Drama and commentary tend to displace narrative.

The latter stages of Lawrence's life in a sense mirror the early stages, constituting a return, with a difference, to where he started from (maybe even, as with Eliot's *Four Quartets*, knowing the place for the first time). Lawrence had moved via Italy to the fictional, even mythic, England of *Lady Chatterley's Lover*, a country ruled over by a maimed Fisher King, like Eliot's 'Waste Land', awaiting the questing Parsifal in the shape of Mellors, the poaching gamekeeper who is peculiarly adept at manipulating cultural and linguistic codes, and has succeeded in extricating himself from a painful marriage where his wife (like Frieda?) was sexually insatiable (whatever that may mean). With this novel, initially entitled *Tenderness*, Lawrence turns his back on the mythologies of political power constructed in *Aaron's Rod*, *The Plumed Serpent*, and *Kangaroo*, exploring instead the power of desire to reach 'the secret places' of life. Steeped in wish fulfilment, however, the novel cannot fail to strike even sympathetic readers as sexist, as Mellors (lovingly and tenderly) in his mythopoeic 'naming of parts' gives Connie back what has always been her own by rights: her body. Lawrence's fascination with the art of the Etruscans,[24] those dark, mysterious 'outsiders' of the Roman world who expressed in their tomb paintings the proximity of life and love to the 'place of excrement' and dissolution, is superimposed upon the English landscape of his youth in a work (extant in three versions, which is a measure of its significance to its author) which briefly became synonymous with sexual outspokenness. Privately published in Italy and distributed to subscribers in order to obviate problems of censorship, it was inevitably greeted in England with the same outrage that had met *The Rainbow* and *Women in Love*. Copies entering England were confiscated by the police, though any number of illicit 'pirate' editions were published. The trouble was partly caused by the four-letter words, which Lawrence hopefully rehabilitates (as if the language really was, as Pound said, in the keeping of 'the damned and despised literati'). More radically disturbing, perhaps, was the fact that Lawrence's novel, a kind of assimilation of *Anna Karenina* to the Raggle-Taggle Gypsies, cannot make up its mind whether it is an encomium of marriage or of adultery. Perhaps this is the real secret of its perennial appeal, but it had witnesses in the notorious trial tying themselves in knots in their endeavours to define 'essential' marriage. From this point in time it looks like a fascinating amalgam of pastoral and romance, with a persistent religious anxiety that generates a mood, and some beautiful poetry, occasionally redolent of *Four Quartets*. It is also an extraordinary postscript, and a very influential one, to that intense, somewhat paranoid, 'critique of culture' that post-Leavisians briefly managed to promote as the only hope for civilisation.

The respiratory weakness from which Lawrence had suffered all his life had now become full-blown tuberculosis; he was, in effect, burnt out, as if from too great an intensity of living. He fought hard against the disease and against those who wanted him to go into hospital, but he eventually succumbed, and entered the Ad Astra Sanatorium at Vence. Like Tolstoy, however, at the approach of death Lawrence had to set out on another journey, and had himself transferred to a private villa in Vence, where he died. He was writing almost up to the end, and in very characteristic terms, about Eric Gill, trying to distinguish Gill's true religious (or prophetic) feelings, expressed in his love of his craft, from his 'tiresome' fussing with words like 'Art and Beauty and God'. Useless to ask, therefore, what the state of Lawrence's soul was when he died, though *A Propos of Lady Chatterley's Lover* furnishes some pretty good clues. Of course it is a cliché to say of someone that 'he died as he lived', especially of someone like Lawrence who seemed to have lived more intensely than others; yet there was always in Lawrence's mind a peculiarly close relationship between life and death, the 'river of life' and the 'river of dissolution'.

2

The Artist as a Young Man

The White Peacock (1911),
The Trespasser (1912), and *Sons and Lovers*
(1913)

'Being an artist' mattered inordinately to Lawrence.[1] The period he grew up in was one of intense intellectual ferment, and it was natural enough that a writer who all his life was something of an autodidact in the best sense of the word should take on a self-consciously 'artistic' mantle in order to distinguish himself, like the young Joyce, from his fellows, and construct an identity different from that given by his provincial environment and parentage. This experience is common enough for any sensitive youngster (cf. Ursula's Tennysonian fantasies in *The Rainbow*). What is remarkable about Lawrence is that he should have been so conscious of the mechanisms of the process in his own case, and used his own fiction early on for the purpose of what he called 'shedding his sicknesses',[2] or in other words investigating his own psychic disorders so as to control them by drawing upon their creative potential. His first two novels take the form of rich repositories of self-generated myths, elaborate evasions, ways of not telling the truth, which are, in their turn, painfully unravelled in *Sons and Lovers* with the help of a rather *ad hoc* Freudianism[3] and a sort of 'anthropological' reading[4] of different modes of experience – religious, social, sexual. *Sons and Lovers* is a Pilgrim's Progress through a *paysage moralisé* of guilt and retribution, the vivid, even lurid, quality of which bears witness to the harshness of the morality, and the intensity of the desire, that generated it. Little seems to temper this Puritanical scrutiny of the emergent self, intent as it is upon scrupulous consistency and integrity (Lawrence's harsh equivalent of Wordsworth's more genial 'growth of a poet's mind'). Yet even here we sometimes seem to be dealing with an elaborately constructed set of alibis – for example for Lawrence's own latent homosexuality – even while we are reading, as many critics have noticed, 'deconstructions' of Oedipal scenarios.[5]

The White Peacock, hard to read through as it is, provides a fascinating range of cultural obfuscations of emotional 'knots' in its subject matter, its imagery and symbolism, its plot structure, and in the way it constructs its narrative positions. The basic material is 'romantic', one might say, meaning, in this context, Victorian-sentimental, in a kind of lesser Pre-Raphaelite pictorial manner (for example the coy reference to Burne-Jones's 'damsels' – are they in distress, perhaps?). In a comment on *Sons and Lovers*, Lawrence described his two earlier novels as 'a decorated idyll running to seed in realism' and a 'florid prose poem', though there is some doubt about which is which. However, Maurice Greiffenhagen's rather kitschy painting *An Idyll* does provide an interesting reference point for *The White Peacock*, for a number of reasons. Most obviously, it is a representation of 'passion'. Of all the late Romantic and decadent works enlisted as cultural totems in the novel, this painting expresses most immediately what is otherwise repressed or suppressed, the power of sexual desire (the novel's more perverse images, like those drawn from Beardsley, are relatively unassimilated). The word 'idyll', therefore, does not seem to relate directly to Nietzsche's use of the term in *The Birth of Tragedy*, though that work and its Wagnerian analogues were to exert a profound influence on *The Trespasser* and beyond. Rather, the Greiffenhagen 'idyll' of *The White Peacock* provides a focus for a fashionable cultural pessimism (Lawrence had read Schopenhauer, Nietzsche's master, with close attention) in which brief glimmers of self-realisation, or fulfilment, (Joyce designated them 'epiphanies') pierce the gloom of a world of violence and destructiveness. This violence is very 'literary', borrowed from Emily Brontë, Hardy, and Meredith, but without any very consistent motivation; it is a set of brooding notations around an obsession, though it foreshadows the 'unstable ego' of *The Rainbow* and *Women in Love*. Greiffenhagen's *Idyll*, a 'swain' embracing a half-reluctant 'nymph', is a correlative for the tormented fantasies of Cyril, the narrator, who is seen as locked into a kind of festering virginity by a social gentility that barely conceals the raw violence of nature. The thesis

is neither subtle nor altogether convincing, but there is a special
interest in the figure of Annable, the gamekeeper, who, like the
artist, patrols the boundaries of nature and culture, and returns, as
a supremely ambivalent but powerful figure, in Lawrence's last
novel, *Lady Chatterley's Lover*. A brief quotation from the opening of
Chapter Three of Part Two, which bears the Meredithian or
Hardyesque title 'The Irony of Inspired Moments' may serve
several purposes at once. It is an instance of what I have called the
'totemistic' use of cultural artefacts (refined upon in the most
remarkable fashion in *The Rainbow* and *Women in Love*); it com-
municates the tentativeness of Cyril, who, as first-person narrator,
is gauchely situated at the centre of events which he could not
properly have been aware of (perhaps an awkward influence from
Wuthering Heights); and it conveys – with a hint of the Lawrence to
come – the rich disorder of a sensibility straining against socially
constructed roles and identities;

> It happened, the next day after the funeral, I came upon a
> reproduction of Beardsley's "Atlanta", and of the tail-piece of
> "Salome", and others. I sat and looked and my soul leaped out
> upon the new thing. I was bewildered, wondering, grudging,
> fascinated. I looked a long time, but my mind, or my soul, would
> come to no state of coherence. I was fascinated and overcome,
> but yet full of stubbornness and resistance.[6]

Cyril's curiously voyeuristic chronicling of the fates of the trio of
lovers, Lettie, Leslie, and George (set up in terms of a Hardyesque
play of opposites, the wrong man inevitably taking up with the
wrong woman, etc.) is a heavily coded search for his own centre of
self. The protagonists, as in Brontë, Hardy, or Dostoevsky, whom
Lawrence was reading at this time, are fragments split off one
'deconstructed' whole. Again the motif of the idyll is significant: it
represents a glimpse of wholeness, a resolution of tensions, the
most powerful being the male/female 'split' that Lawrence experienced acutely not only as frustrated desire but also within his own
psyche. It is also, as a version of pastoral, a momentary polarisation
of the destructive forces of nature; such moments are recorded
elsewhere in the novel with great affection and sensitivity in the
form of the festivals and rituals of the community which mediate
between the indifference of the cosmos and man's brief
blossoming.[7]

What holds one's attention in the novel, then, is not so much its thin 'romantic' plot, as its obsessive foregrounding, with intermittent but vivid psychological insight, of the components of that plot. The tenuous identity of the dramatised narrator, for instance, keeps breaking up. Doubled at some points with a kind of soul mate in his homoerotic attraction to George, he is attracted at other points, and strangely subjected, to the ambiguously 'transgressive' father-figure Annable, who, with a kind of perverse authority, speaks, in dialect, the Schopenhauerian language of cultural pessimism and mysogyny. The author/narrator is also engaged in a kind of secret rite aimed at the degradation and death of the 'natural' father, who is boldly given the maiden name of Lawrence's *mother*, Beardsall. These fragments of what is surely the real 'plot' put one in mind of Lawrence's later, much more systematic and meaningful, deconstruction of the 'old stable ego' of the character in *The Rainbow* and *Women in Love*.

The more closely we scrutinise these energised fragments, the more enigmatic they appear. Getting rid of his father, old 'Frenchy', by having him drink himself to death, was doubtless a consoling fantasy for the young Lawrence, who on the evidence here did not know what he was doing, or if he did would not share the secret with the callow Cyril. But we also see the powerful fascination exerted by the Modernist construction of a culture which is more real than the civilisation which engenders it, and which offers an alternative father. One privileged component of this culture, especially in the German tradition, with which Lawrence identified particularly closely at this time, is the 'folk', thinly disguised in working-class vernacular. Herein lies Lawrence's ambivalence towards the split father-image in the novel. Annable (a curiously androgynous name) is a Dionysiac or Cthonic figure, one of those lords of life and death whose praises Lawrence later sang in *The Plumed Serpent*, a tragic figure in a secular and increasingly 'feminine' civilisation (the young Lawrence's fear of women finds an easy outlet in Annable's 'proletarian' hatred of the genteel white peacock of the title: perhaps a projection of Lawrence's unconscious hatred of his mother). Like other Modernist constructions of this elusive and more 'real' reality, it can be recognised unmistakably by the fact that it is lost, or survives in such a heavily coded form that one must join a select group of initiates in order to grasp it.

The same may be said of *The Trespasser*, a more coherent work, which has recently been filmed with an intelligent script by Hugh Stoddart. Frank Kermode described it as 'fashionably Wagnerian', and noted its 'Ninety-ish' prose.[8] Ford Madox Ford called it 'a rotten work of genius'. Beginning as a simple 'idyll', worked up from a manuscript by Helen Corke, about a musician who (temporarily) leaves his wife for an illicit holiday with a pupil, it ends in a very 'seedy' (borrowing Lawrence's term) Dostoevskian realism with the suicide of the protagonist, Siegmund. *En route, The Trespasser* brushes with some large cultural issues. The Nietzschean and Wagnerian components of the text lead us into questions about the death of tragedy in a secular age, and explore, as Nietzsche did, the possibility of its resurrection (he said birth, but no matter) from the 'spirit of music'. There is an attempt, again Hardyesque or Brontëesque, to see Man (and, naturally, woman) as the plaything of the gods rather than simply as a social being. Myth codes a range of ambiguities (male/female, subject/object, domestic/erotic, individual/collective, and so forth) and mediates between the known and the unknown. The language of the novel has a 'musical' density of texture much richer than that of *The White Peacock*, since it is built upon the Apollo/Dionysus split which forms the basis of *The Birth of Tragedy*, whereby the world exists under two aspects: as it is experienced, and as it is known (or, in Schopenhauer's terms, as 'Will', the force that flows through us and in which we are immersed, and as 'Idea' or representation, the way we image things to ourselves). In Nietzsche's view, there has belatedly been what he calls a 'gradual awakening of the Dionysian spirit in the modern world', especially in Germany, that emergent nation (Lawrence called it 'adolescent') where a tragic 'modern' vision is struggling to be reborn from out of the contemporary secular world view. It is the art of Apollo, maker of symbols, that mediates the Dionysiac vision embodied in music, expressing the pulse of the universe and the rhythms of our own organisms; but the representation is not the thing represented, the Word is not the World, because to confront 'reality' directly would be equivalent to madness, the final dissolution of the Self:

> We imagine we see only Tristan, motionless, asking himself dully: "The old tune, why does it wake me?" ... However powerfully pity affects us it nevertheless saves us in a way from

the primordial suffering of the world, just as the symbolic image of the myth saves us from the immediate perception of the highest world-idea, just as thought and word save us from the uninhibited effusions of the unconscious will.[9]

The profound significance of the Wagnerian music-drama for Nietzsche (until he fell out with Wagner's religiosity and took a fancy to *Carmen*) thus lay in the fact that, like Greek tragedy, it 'avails itself of the word', but also that, again, like Greek tragedy, it can 'place beside it the basis and origin of the word'. Nietzsche condemns modern philosophers for substituting ethical questions (as Aristotle, especially in his *Poetics*, substituted formal questions) for aesthetic questions. The aesthetic, for Nietzsche, is defined by its transgression of the boundaries of good and evil. The appeal of this position to the young Lawrence, trying to negotiate the constraints of provincial English nonconformism, is readily apparent. Pain and discord are at the heart of experience (Lawrence was having a bad time in 1912) but tragic art is (as Lawrence himself later put it) 'a great kick at misery':

> The joy aroused by the tragic myth has the same origin as the joyous sensation of dissonance in music. The Dionysian, with its primordial joy experienced even in pain, is the common source of music and tragic myth.[10]

This idea permeates Modernism in both theory and practice, from its 'heroic' formulation here and (for example) in the work of Yeats (who understood exactly what Lawrence meant by calling *Lady Chatterley's Lover* a tragedy)[11] to its domestication in the 'irony' and 'ambiguity' beloved of the New Criticism.

There is a plethora of references to Wagner in *The Trespasser*, motivated on the plot level by the fact that Siegmund plays fiddle in an opera house orchestra, and on the symbolic level by the fact that the world of the novel is a fallen world waiting for its Siegfried, or heroic deliverer: will Siegmund and Helena (Sieglinde) make the grade? The motifs of Wotan's anger and of the dragon are referred to, in association with what is called 'the call of the horn across the sea of Tristan' (presumably the plangent *cor anglais* melody at the beginning of Act Three of Wagner's opera). A few pages later there is an allusion to 'the Grail music in *Lohengrin*'. The

Ring is evoked several times: sometimes the whole context embodies the allusion (as in the passage evoking the moaning of the wind 'like the calling of many violoncellos' which suggests the prelude to *Walküre*), sometimes the reference is *en passant* (for example where Helena alludes to Wotan's clumsiness – 'He knocks over the bowl, and flap-flap-flap go the gaping fishes, *pizzicato*' – an elliptical reference to the Rhinemaidens, who are often called 'fish'). There is a concrete allusion to 'the bird music out of *Siegfried*' and to 'the Spring Song from *Die Walküre*', as well as (oddly) 'the well-known movement from the Valkyrie Ride'. The defensively off-hand 'well-known' in the last allusion suggests that Lawrence takes a strictly limited interest in Wagner's complex structures; indeed, the *Lietmotiven* are treated almost as folk songs.

As with *The White Peacock*, we are made aware of the mask-play, the intricate displacements, afforded by the symbolic models invoked, the cultural totemism, within or behind which there is a tense, unfocused, erotic strife. Siegmund, like Cyril, is more acted upon than acting, a fact underlined by the frequency of impersonal agents: 'Sieglinde's island drew nearer and nearer'; 'Houses crowded down to the shore to meet him'; 'the sky's dark shipping pressed closer and closer'; 'Siegmund watched the platform, shiny with rain, slide past'. The tale shows us that Siegmund's fatal passivity lies at the root of the tragedy as much as, if not more than, Helena's 'Apollonian' immunity to the world of passion.

Wagner's chromatic music heralds the dissolution of tonality, which is also the merging of subject with object. His discords are as plangent as they are because in the end there is actually nowhere for them to resolve. The same may be said of the relationship between Siegmund and Helena, and of Siegmund's inner strife. Lawrence's appropriation of this 'new' tragic aesthetic, like Nietzsche's 'birth' of tragedy, is, for all its fascinating transcoding of the Hellenic world, shot through with the psychologism which its German original affects to despise. After Wagner, and building on Wagner, Schoenberg had to devise a new system, based on an odd sort of democracy in which every note was equal to every other. After *The Trespasser*, and building on Nietzsche, Lawrence had to rethink his 'metaphysic', or philosophy of art, in the *Study of Thomas Hardy* and *The Crown*, and the two great novels, *The Rainbow* and *Women in Love*, which implement this metaphysic. The Wagnerian aesthetic, like other Modernist creeds, leads first to solipsism, then inevitably returns to the Christianity from which it emerged. Lawrence's Wagnerian 'idyll' leads to 'seedy' realism, and death, as the family (Lawrence's own?) closes in. As in *The White Peacock*, there is a dream of nebulous unity, the polarisation of tension: but the cult of death, the death wish, in this novel is much stronger, probably as a consequence of the illness and death of Lawrence's mother, though this is never made explicit. The Apollonian Helena continues to place her trust in 'the spirit of music', even after the sardonic little episode of their meeting with Hampson:

> All along Fate had been resolving, from the very beginning, resolving obvious discords, gradually, by unfamiliar progression; and out of original combinations weaving wondrous harmonies with our lives. Really, the working-out has been wondrous, is wondrous now. The Master-Fate is too great an artist to suffer an anti-climax. I am sure the Master-Musician is too great an artist to allow a bathetic anti-climax.

The irony of Helena's consoling fictions needs no underlining. Kermode speaks of a 'cult of castration, euphemistically described', but this scarcely does justice to Lawrence's decorative fusion of Golden Bough-ish mythologies with Flower Maidens out of *Parsifal*, Persephone, etc. The cultural overkill is equalled only by the intricate evasions already mentioned. The most powerfully evoked sexual experience in the novel, after all, is the 'fusing in a kiss', but the reticence in this area, which is experienced as a major issue, is attributed to the fact that Helena, or so we are told, belongs to 'that class of "dreaming women" with whom passion exhausts itself at the mouth'. The sea and the moon serve her sad, passive beauty, and it is her 'new, softy beauty' which she gives to Siegmund as 'the earth in which his strange flowers grew' (the recent film handled this with admirable tact). But the powerful symbolism of the novel keeps telling a different and more convincing tale. In Chapter Six, Siegmund injures himself swimming; 'he caught his thigh on a sharp submerged point' (a strikingly inappropriate phrase) and then dismisses it: 'It was nothing'. The wound seems self-inflicted, the implementation of a death wish. This episode is paralleled in Chapter Eight, where Siegmund finds a white cave 'brilliant and full of life as mounting sap' (at least, that is one reading of Lawrence's deliberately 'chromatic' syntax here):

Siegmund had found a white cave welling with green water,
brilliant and full of life as mounting sap. The white rock
glimmered through the water, and soon Siegmund shimmered
also in the living green of the sea, like pale flowers trembling
upward.

He swims through an archway 'into a passage where the water ran
like a flood of green light over the skin-white bottom' (*sic!*); 'he
waded out of the green, cold water on to sand that was as pure as
the shoulders of Helena'; 'Sand that was as soft and warm as white
fur'; 'a white virgin blossom'; 'The warm body of the shore' – it is
clear enough that Siegmund is enacting in fantasy the consumma-
tion of his passion, and equally that 'nature' (actually a densely
coded symbolism) has supplanted Helena (who is waiting for him
in the garden of the house where they are staying). The imagery of
initiation, of explicit penetration, closes oddly – but at one level
altogether convincingly – with Siegmund playing with the sand
'like a child playing some absorbing game with itself'. The delight
of this 'decadent' writing is that Lawrence seems to have no idea of
what is really going on. To his reader, the polymorphous play has
already supplanted sexual love even before the process of self-
laceration begins. The last image of the equivocal and regressive
mythic sequence occurs in Chapter Seventeen, where Siegmund
goes back to 'his little bay'. He fancies it full of 'sea-women with
dark locks, and young sea-girls' (cf. that other Modernist castration
fantasy, Eliot's 'Prufrock'). The tide carries him through the
'skin-white, full-fleshed wall of the archway' and he grazes his arm
on a rock: he accuses himself of being 'careless'. Helena meanwhile
explores the rock-pools.

    Whatever Lawrence intended (and I do not think he knew what
he intended), Siegmund's erotic delight is equated with a death
wish, and the images of the 'secret passage' leading to his bay are
images not of birth and renewal, but of regression, accompanied by
symbolic castration (guilt). 'The tide carried him through the high
gate into the porch': it is striking how often domestic imagery,
images of houses and of homes, are associated with Siegmund's
tragedy. Evidently the little group of children in Chapter Seven are
deliberately 'planted' there (like that odd light bulb washed up by
the sea) to remind Siegmund of his responsibility to his own family.
Do the domestic images resist all attempts to relate them to the

intense 'cultural' domain? Perhaps they represent a different dimension of the same tragedy, but it is as well to remind ourselves that George Steiner said of *Tristan*, with chilling accuracy, that it is 'A drawing-room triangle on a cosmic scale'.[12] Francis Fergusson notes that 'many have tried to interpret *Tristan* as only a symptom of the disturbances in Wagner's own psyche following his thwarted affair with Frau Wesendonck'.[13] The music makes this impossible, yet the 'psychologism' of which I have spoken is never absent from Wagner's tragedy, militating against his vaunted reintroduction of tragic experience into the public/universal/social realm. Fergusson makes this point rather well, in relation to Nietzsche:

> A man who has put his ear to the heart-chamber of the cosmic will ... would he not collapse at once? Could he endure, in the wretched fragile tenement of the human individual, to hear the re-echo of countless cries of joy and sorrow from 'the vast void of cosmic night', without flying irresistibly to his primitive home?' The direct answer to Nietzsche's rhetorical question would be that, when the curtain falls on Act 3, one does in fact catch the subway towards one's unprimitive home, such as it is – unutterably feeble and discouraged, perhaps, but a wretched human individual still.[14]

This more or less follows the dynamics of Lawrence's plot, except that Lawrence's 'trespasser' cannot, in one sense, ever go home again. The Puritan morality that Lawrence inherited leads him to a conclusion that resolves the tragedy in a blend of Ibsen and Dostoevsky, far removed from the 'idyll'. Siegmund 'castrates' himself for his 'trespass'; and then commits suicide. The human fails to become divine. The redemptive figure (Siegfried) fails to make his ordained appearance in order to defy Fricka's anathematising of the transgression, by the lovers, of the taboo on incest. On his way home, Siegmund's steamer nearly runs down a family pleasure boat; the mother on board behaves with striking calm, appearing 'as one who watched the sources of life, saw it great and impersonal'. Siegmund's return is a striking blow-up of Lawrence's father coming back from a drinking bout, though old Lawrence would never have had the grace to hang himself. Having entered the domain of wish-fulfilment, we remain there. Byrne, the jokey, earthy, but always sensitive Lawrence figure, leads Helena to fresh pastures – 'I always like the gold-green of cut fields, they seem to give off sunshine even when the sky's greyer than a tabby cat.' But the real issues shaping the fictional world of the novel cannot be worked out until *Sons and Lovers* has done its job of helping Lawrence to 'shed his sickness'.

It is odd that *Sons and Lovers* has been so little discussed for what it essentially is, a *Kunstlerroman*. The elaborate aestheticism of the first two novels is here analysed and 'placed' to an extent; but we can still clearly see that Lawrence's doctrine of 'art for my sake' may quite properly be interpreted as an extreme form of dandyism, since it implies actually *living out* what Yeats called 'the perfection of the work' with a sometimes frightening, deranged intensity. At all events, *Sons and Lovers* indisputably charts the growth of the artist's mind, and it is a process as relentless as in Joyce's *Portrait of the Artist*, in the course of which innocent people get hurt – most notably the girl who tries hard to love and help him – without any very obvious signs of remorse on the hero's or the author's part. Lawrence acknowledged Paul's 'priggishness' as his own; but such simple moral terms are an evasion. The novel is a Modernist 'myth of the birth of the hero' (to borrow Otto Rank's title),[15] and works through the clusters of neurotic symptoms displayed and aestheticised in the two earlier novels, as its protagonist fights for his life against the death-drive in himself, in his society, and in the 'culture' that both is and is not the 'answer' to the oppressive family drama. It goes without saying, perhaps, that its influence on English literature has been incalculable. More than that, it is a key text in the formation of a particularly seductive, though in many ways radically misleading, Puritan critique of contemporary culture of the kind I mentioned in my Preface.

The battle to possess the cultural 'means of production' is apparent from the first page of the novel (parodied by David Storey, one of the few legitimate heirs to the Lawrence legacy, in his masterly *A Prodigal Child*). Situating his family in terms of the prevailing social codes, the author introduces at the same time the image of the gin-pit donkey turning endlessly in circles. The writing has a sharpness of definition (which Lawrence almost immediately took against, as being over-full of 'sensation and presentation'), that marks it off quite startlingly from the uncertain conclusion to *The Trespasser*; the donkey functions well as both realistic detail and as symbol. Similarly, the 'geography' of the miner's house is, as surely as the domestic setting of *A Portrait of the Artist*, a labyrinth to be transcended as well as an exact notation of environment and circumstance. Initially, the transgressor is the mother: the image of the woman looking disconsolately out through the window, picked up from Victorian fiction, will be transmuted into a full-blown theory of what Leavis called 'essential English history' in *The Rainbow*: 'I wait, and what I wait for can never come.' The class antagonism of the parents is transformed early in the novel into a psycho-sexual polarisation of mythic dimensions, a battle between flesh and spirit, an image of the Fall or what Eliot called the 'dissociation of sensibility'.

Lawrence was beginning to understand his (our?) judgemental culture well, and how it had affected his emotional growth, and he constantly hits off perfect encapsulations of it: 'She could not be content with the little he might be; she would have him the much that he ought to be' – a proposition about education, among other things, that goes to the heart of the strengths and the weaknesses (a 'Leavisian' phrase!) of the grammar school ethos that formed Lawrence. Are the women the 'responsible' element (among a bunch of irresponsible hard-drinking men?). As guardians of the moral order, on the other hand, are they not a corrosive presence in the life of their menfolk? Lawrence, at all events, shows his mother as the *Kulturträger*, not only because of her interest in books and ideas and her membership of the Womens' Guild, but also because of her defence of 'values'; and the result is an ambivalent image of Woman that he could never quite get out of his mind: like Arnold's Culture in an age of Anarchy, or like John the Baptist preaching in the desert, she prepares the way for the Light, the Word, the coming of the Son, the Great Atoner; but the price she exacts for this service is exorbitant.

It is, therefore, central to Lawrence's image of the Mother that she is *excluded* by the powerful male (Mrs Morel is shut out in the garden by her drunken husband: drunkenness equals the irrational exercise of power) and impregnated not by any 'mere' man but by the Holy Spirit. At Paul's conception (his Scriptural name is not accidental, St Paul being in many ways the first Puritan) the heavens are full of portents, as at the birth of any hero: is it not the artist who is the real hero of our time? Inevitably, their most immediate ancestry is Christian: the Anglican revival plus Arts and Crafts. The (Pre-Raphaelite) white lilies filled with moonlight shed their scent, and their yellow pollen, restoring Gertrude's emotional and spiritual equilibrium after the conflict with her husband. Just as the local minister earns her pity ('his young wife is dead; that is why he makes his love into the Holy Ghost') so she, too, takes strength from God and transmits it directly to the young child ('She thrust the infant forward to the crimson, throbbing sun, almost with relief'). Paul's closeness to his mother (a navel string that 'had not been broken') is underscored when he is 'baptised in blood' (in a family row, Morel throws a drawer at her, which cuts her forehead, the blood dripping on Paul). In a brief lull, another child, Arthur, is conceived – notably without the portents and omens that accompanied Paul's birth – and the older boy, William, begins to move out into the world. In this world of men, which is run from behind the scenes by the possessive mother, as is still the way in many countries (especially the Catholic countries Lawrence was attracted to) the girls – sister Annie, for example – seem to count for very little: and in a Gothic image, with an anthropological dimension perhaps derived from Frazer, Paul first 'accidentally' jumps 'crash into the face' of her favourite doll, and then, as if to destroy the evidence of his guilty act, proposes making a sacrifice of it.

Whether or not this incident is autobiographical (and *Sons and Lovers*, like *A Portrait of the Artist*, makes creative play with the 'gaps' between autobiography and fiction), it offers an exceptionally powerful image of a latent resentment against women, and maybe even that Baudelairean wish not to have been born that figures elsewhere in the novel (*Les Fleurs de Mal* was a formative influence on Lawrence, though the proper place to study this would be in connection with *Women in Love*). The fact that 'Paul hated his father', and is acutely embarrassed, when he collects his father's wages, at having to answer to his father's name, 'small and inadequate', cannot altogether, in its Oedipal resonances, account for this degradation of women. Certainly we hear much of the Son who is his mother's surrogate Lover, and the mother who delights in being courted, like a sweetheart, making Paul's relationship with Miriam virtually impossible; his life story becomes 'an Arabian Nights ... told night after night to his mother'. But we also see many significant instances of the young Paul growing as an artist by virtue of his mother's waning powers (with some of Mellors' divine aplomb he 'names the world' for her: 'his heart hurt with love, seeing her hand, used with work, holding the little bunch of flowers he gave her'); and we see Paul choosing, especially after William's terrifying seduction and death, to channel his libido into the domain of creative, priest-like spiritual intensity rather than towards (and in fact even significantly *against*) the female.

Jessie Chambers understood this better than Lawrence, when she wrote her memoirs.[16] From the start of their relationship, she was 'a maiden in bondage', and as with Sir John Millais's much admired painting *The Knight Errant* (1870), we are left with serious doubts about the intentions of the heavily armoured knight towards the bound and virtually naked girl. As with this painting, however, what is being represented is essentially a kind of *stasis* of desire (cf. Keat's 'Ode on a Grecian Urn'). 'Lad-and-Girl Love' is already an ironic title for a romance based on priestly instruction, initiation, and Biblical 'revelation' (when Paul paints pine-trees, they must of necessity become 'God's burning bush'). Miriam's soulfulness may have been real enough, given her upbringing; but the novel shows us clearly that Paul needs to hold on to the idea of her vulnerability in order to confirm his power as the bringer of the Holy Spirit, the divine mystery to be worshipped, which lies altogether 'beyond' her, even though it thrives on her humble adulation. Why must learning be so violent? – it is a kind of violence endemic to our Puritan culture, perhaps, as Lawrence tries to tell us in *The Rainbow* and 'The Education of the People', but it is also the Baudelairean violence of the creative imagination, close to psychosis in such poems as *A celle qui est trop gaie*. It is here, precisely, that we enter the 'paysage moralisé', where a rose-bush, 'yew-hedges and borders of yellow crocuses', an old umbrella, the moon, Gothic arches, are charged with such significance. He, Paul, the artist-as-God, new-creates the world, and for this a woman is needed, a muse. At the same time, it is important to protect this pristine, visionary creation from the 'contamination' of the woman: 'When she bent and breathed a flower, it was as if she and the flower were loving each other. Paul hated her for it.' For the (male) Modernist, every 'femme' is 'fatale': especially, perhaps, the yielding kind. This truth cannot come out into the open, though in the most 'confessional' passages there is a hint of it:

He did not know himself what was the matter. He was naturally so young, and their intimacy was so abstract, he did not know he wanted to crush her on to his breast to ease her ache there. He was afraid of her.

It is only superficially true that the unacknowledged problem is one of suppressed desire: the 'self-tormentor', to use Baudelaire's term,[17] who makes poetry from the ecstasy of martyrdom, is Paul himself.

If one needed confirmation of this, one would only have to look at the way those thoroughly 'secular' lovers, Vulcan and Venus, enter the tale, in the form of Baxter and Clara Dawes (the agent of 'free love', the emancipated woman, and her husband the factory smith, 'making the irons for cripple instruments' – a phrase worth pondering!). Like all such 'emancipated' Venuses, Clara is, of course, waiting for a 'real' man, a commanding Mars-like figure: it is another version of the Andromeda myth, with Paul to play Perseus, as well as another Oedipal scenario in which the odds are not stacked so heavily against the Son. In this case, however, Paul can dispense with the need for 'trampling his ideas' on the 'threshing-floor' of a woman's mind and body, because the woman in question lacks the 'mystery' of the sacrificial victim: the following passage deserves to be quoted at length, since it gives an interesting twist to the 'chivalric' imagery:

"What a treat to be a knight," he said, "and to have a pavilion here".

"And to have us shut up safely?" replied Clara.

"Yes," he answered, "singing with your maids at your broidery. I would carry your banner of white and green and heliotrope. I would have 'W.S.P.U.' emblazoned on my shield, beneath a woman rampant."

"I have no doubt," said Clara, "that you would much rather fight for a woman than let her fight for herself."

"I would. When she fights for herself she seems like a dog before a looking-glass, gone into a mad fury with its own shadow."

"And *you* are the looking-glass?" she asked, with a curl of the lip.

"Or the shadow," he replied.

"I am afraid," she said, "that you are too clever."

"Well, I leave it to you to be *good*," he retorted, laughing. "Be good, sweet maid, and just let *me* be clever."

But Clara wearied of his flippancy. Suddenly, looking at her, he saw that the upward lifting of her face was misery and not scorn. His heart grew tender for everybody. He turned and was gentle with Miriam, whom he had neglected till then.[18]

The uneasy ironic play with the still-fashionable Arthurian imagery speaks volumes about Lawrence's sado-masochistic make-up. Clara constitutes no threat to the integrity of the artist; she is in evident need of instant emotional and imaginative 'deliverance', but being married does not ask for any long-term commitment. In an interesting variation on the seduction theme she releases Paul from the burden of his virginity (though it is comic to compare the elaborately symbolic, almost sacramental, version of this in the chapter called 'Passion', with the mundane facts of the matter as reported by Alice Dax). But she is nevertheless being used. What Paul remains faithful to is actually the Muse, a role for which the pragmatic Clara does not qualify; and Miriam is made to connive at the whole thing, being sure of her own hold on him:

> Miriam knew how strong was the attraction of Clara for him; but still she was certain that the best in him would triumph. His feeling for Mrs. Dawes – who, moreover, was a married woman – was shallow and temporal, compared with his love for herself.

The crucially placed chapter called 'The Test on Miriam' actually registers Paul's morbid dread of sexual love. The real test is on Paul; and he is not so much found wanting, as discovered never to have wanted love in the first place. All the emotional energy of the chapter goes once again into the incandescent 'natural' description (a lurid kind of displacement), and the opening of Chapter Twelve cathects Paul's desire into the 'figures in a landscape' of his work as an artist. It is in this chapter that Lawrence points forward to *The Rainbow* by telling Clara (Frieda?) about the 'pillar of cloud by day and pillar of fire by night' of Genesis: as a boy, he thought these referred to the pit, 'with its steam, and its lights, and the burning bank – and I thought the Lord was always at the pit-top'. In this chapter, too, he refers back to his holiday with his mother on the Isle of Wight (relevant, surely, to *The Trespasser*). The 'passion' of which the chapter speaks is as much Christ's passion (or Lawrence's crucifixion into selfhood) as it is desire for Clara (here again, there is a strong suggestion of ritual sacrifice about the coming together of the lovers). It only remains for Paul to dispose of the secondary 'father figure', Baxter. Like Beardsall and Siegmund, he is degraded and dismissed; and eventually Clara has to be cast off too; but not before Lawrence has made some remarkable forays into his own psycho-sexual make-up as he explores the gradual decline of his feelings for her.

The trauma described as experienced by Paul on the death of his mother is strongly autobiographical; Lawrence, indeed, had a kind of breakdown, which took the overt form of a physical rather than a mental illness, but which is nevertheless registered in *Sons and Lovers* as severe depression. Like Ursula in *The Rainbow*, he recovered, with his extraordinary power of rising from the dead, and the confident end of *Sons and Lovers* makes it look as if his life and his writings so far had been leading up to this moment; but things would not have gone so well if he had not met Frieda in 1912. *Sons and Lovers* would itself have been substantially different: Frieda's knowledge of Freudian psychiatry, however 'amateur', helped to structure the novel; and although Lawrence objected to reductive Freudian readings there is no doubt that the theory of the Oedipus complex has been drawn upon extensively as a heuristic device (and to some extent as a sort of camouflage). Lawrence was fortunate enough to have met, at the right moment, the woman who could illuminate his 'cultural' struggle from a completely new angle, and give him that large 'alien' perspective on his own experience that *The Rainbow* bodies forth.

3

'Essential English history'?
The Rainbow

Walter Benjamin wrote of Charles Baudelaire, the first great 'Modernist', that he had been 'cheated out of his experience'; this was what gave his (often obscure) work representativeness, and made him a 'typical modern man'.[1] Unpacking Benjamin's gnomic utterances is never straightforward, but his 'far-fetched' conceits always turn out to have been worth the carriage. The French poet (who appears at crucial points in *Sons and Lovers* and has left a deep impress upon *Women in Love*, which might almost be subtitled *Fleurs du Mal*) was a more extreme case than Lawrence of the psychic damage, as well as the creative drive, attributable to the Oedipus complex. When, after the death of his father, his mother married General Aupick, Baudelaire was perhaps not literally 'cheated', but he was actually debarred from the patrimony which he had thought of as his by rights. His consequent hatred of his stepfather, and resentment towards his mother, coloured all his adult relations with women. Closer to the surface of Benjamin's conceit, however, is a half-articulated sociocultural thesis, followed through in a number of his essays, to the effect that the writer has become, in the modern world, not just a supplier of commodities, but a commodity himself. Urbanisation, undermining community life and 'traditional' ties of family and relationship, throws the individual back upon his own resources. While this accelerating process of change discloses all the fascinating possibilities of a 'plural', manufactured, promiscuous and disposable world, it makes it harder, at the same time, to experience one's life as an organic whole. The question of what a life means, of what it is 'worth', is one that has traditionally exercised the writer, from Homer's *Odyssey* (not to mention the Bible) to the present day. Now that works of art are mechanically reproducible and disseminated far and wide (also 'recycled' in various ways) they have to work much harder, as Benjamin tells us, to maintain their authority (Kafka's work is preoccupied with the trauma of 'displaced' authority virtually to the exclusion of everything else). Much of Baudelaire's work is consciously located, as Benjamin rightly observes, in a universe where 'wisdom' is dying out, and it is given over to 'filling in the blanks' in history, to 'synthesising' an aura of uniqueness, of subjectivity, of unrepeatability (the Symbolist aesthetic; but also much else in Modernism, which as a movement is made in the image of Narcissus). In the end it is neither history nor psychology (in whatever sense) that maintains the continuity of the self. This increasingly elusive entity, as Benjamin perceives it, is upheld by faith; Benjamin's own faith is a fascinating blend of Marxism and Judaism. In his work, as in Kafka's work, writing, which in our time must be seen as the trace left by the archetypal victim, may also bring the only hope of atonement. It has actually become, as even the secular Arnold clearly foresaw, the last refuge of the numinous.

Benjamin, one of the last great practitioners of Modernist hermeneutics, and later Mikhail Bakhtin, the theoretician of the dialogic principle,[2] may together help us to open up significant dimensions of Lawrence's *The Rainbow* and *Women in Love*. Frank Kermode appositely used the word 'palimpsest' in reference to these texts:[3] we are very conscious in reading *The Rainbow* of a process of 'layering' as the experience of one generation is super-imposed upon, and tested against, that of another. Novels, of course, have their own way of constructing a finite continuum of time from their 'beginning' to their 'end'. Fiction is necessarily linear; but the time-philosophies of Modernism remind us that the clock and the calendar are arbitrary devices for chopping up and pinning down existence. We do not 'feel' time simply as successive-ness; Bergson, for example in *Creative Evolution* and half a dozen other influential books, constructs time as flow, with an inter-penetration of past, present and future, and proposes that history is something we are immersed in. Lawrence urged us to 'live fully on the spot where we are', but no writer is more aware of the truth of the fact that at any given moment we are not only what we are but also what we were and what we will become. The Modernist fascination with 'unfinishedness' (taken over from Romantic art and literature) stems from a verifiable conviction that, subjectively speaking, the psyche is 'layered' temporally, a space–time continuum. Its density may be constructed in various ways; one is that of Proust's 'involuntary memory', another is Nietzsche's eternal return, or the Freudian unconscious in which past experiences are stored and interact with the present. And even if we are commonsensically suspicious of (for example) Bergson's idealism, which certainly makes heavy demands on what Polanyi called 'personal knowledge',[4] the social and absolute sciences offer a partial reinforcement of Modernist constructions of time by the attention they give, at the turn of the century, to the crucial role of subjectivity or relativity in what 'common sense' had taken to be nothing more or less than 'objective' observation. Even Marx, that great teleological thinker, sardonically conceded, with reference to Baudelaire's *bête noire*, Napoleon III, that history repeated itself, the first time as tragedy, the second time as farce. All sons, of course, set out to displace their fathers, and Modernist literature is conceived under the sign of this inexorable Oedipal process. But equally, in the community and in the individual, a deterministic code (genetic, familial, historical) condemns us all to repeat, with a few differences, the 'mistakes' (or the parapraxes) of our forebears.

One of the wonders of Lawrence's *The Rainbow* is the strength of the principle of hope that keeps its author out of Proust's cork-lined room of obsessive retrospection (or, indeed, the padded cell, though Lawrence thought sometimes, especially during the war, that he was close to it) in the fact of the knowledge that time does not stand still and lost time cannot 'really' be recaptured (and may be, as Eliot feared, 'unredeemable') things will nevertheless be no better for Ursula than they were for Anna or Lydia, while in many ways, for the thinking and sensitive individual, life has become immeasurably harder. It is also no accident that many of Lawrence's hard-pressed protagonists are women.

We are required to read *The Rainbow*, therefore, both backwards and sideways, as well as according to the old linear logic, and to respond to the ways in which it 'spatialises' time, if we want to do justice to the techniques which the different episodes use to spark off new resonances from the Wagnerian *Leitmotiven* that run through the whole text (derived from the initial rainbow = cloud plus fire, broken circle, cathedral arch, etc., pattern). The strong forward thrust is thus complicated by cyclical patterns of time, corresponding to the 'widening circles' of civilisation in a rapidly

industrialising society, but also recapitulating, in the destinies of
individuals, the experience of what Lawrence liked to call 'the race
– as it were'.[5] The effect of 'density' is increased most notably by
the different uses of scripture in the novel: as paradigm, as
intertext, as lost wisdom, as a vast repository of images, etc.
Unsurprisingly, Lawrence had trouble explaining to his (very
intelligent) publisher's reader, Edward Garnett, what he was aim-
ing at, and had to write him a long letter touching on many
preoccupations which we can now see as representative of Modernism in the arts. It has been quoted many times:

> You must not look in my novel for the old stable ego – of the
> character. There is another *ego*, according to whose action the
> individual is unrecognisable, and passes through, as it were,
> allotropic states which it needs a deeper sense than any we've
> been used to exercise to discover are states of the same single
> radically unchanged element.[6]

Lawrence's tortuous Nietzschean argument goes on to relegate the
social and 'ethical' dimension of character to a secondary order of
things, asserting that the really interesting component, the novelist's true 'theme', is some constant element (he calls it 'carbon', i.e.
the radical element of life) located deeper than mere 'personality',
which is no more than the changing 'allotropic states' of this
chemical element, made manifest as coal or soot or diamond, as
heroes and villains, in the 'social' order. We are again in the realm
of Apollo and Dionysus, the world as 'Will' (experience) and as
'Idea' (representation), building upon Nietzsche's 'aesthetic' thesis
in *The Birth of Tragedy* (and perhaps Rimbaud's schizoid 'je est un
autre').[7] The hardest thing, in the distracted modern world, is to
take hold of the continuity of one's own experience, to possess it
with any degree of fullness or authenticity.

  The writer's heroism (and all-pervasive sense of tragedy) consists
in his dedication to the pursuit of this 'essential history' as he (I
wanted to write s/he, but this *is* a masculinist thesis) painfully
registers continuity in and through change, exposing himself to a
succession of 'destabilising' shifts of focus. His gift of interpretation
consists above all in his responsiveness to the plurality of voices
unleashed by the art of writing: Scriptural (with a range of
sermons, litanies, prayers, lives of saints, and anathemas); Cultural

(*The Rainbow* situates its characters and its 'plot' in relation to changing phases of sensibility mediated through Ruskin, Carlyle, Morris, Arnold, *et al.*); and Sexual (since the whole argument of *The Rainbow* is caught up with the politics of gender, and we should not underemphasise emergent feminism as a powerful force 'destabilising' the 'old ego' of Victorian civilisation). Lawrence's tone in this letter is necessarily placatory; but the substance of his argument, as well as the great pair of novels to which this letter relates, are not so reassuring. We have come very close in important respects to Benjamin's arguments about wisdom draining out of the world (and sometimes in Lawrence we are not a million miles away from Kafka's paranoid fables about meaning seeping away towards, or being supplanted by, the 'female').[8] Yet there is (as with Benjamin and Baudelaire) another side to this awed perception of crisis. As the unitary, patriarchal authority crumbles, the 'gap' it leaves to be filled in by writing becomes more and more richly suggestive. The great Victorian agnostics had taken upon themselves the moral burden of constructing a secular faith, but it was left for Lawrence and some of the other writers we call Modernist to go further and preside over the inauguration of a new mythology of the end of time.

The Modernist 'sense of an ending', to borrow Kermode's title, throws, in turn, a special emphasis on beginnings. The opening of *The Rainbow* shows us how we inevitably construct our myths of origins out of our sense of what is missing here and now. Doubtless Epic has always fulfilled this function, whether sacred (like the Bible, which has a rather striking beginning) or secular. Freud gave a new impetus to myths of origins, with his revival of Oedipus as well as the whole psychoanalytic process of recuperating lost time; indeed, it has often been pointed out that Modernism as a whole is time-obsessed. The opening of *The Rainbow*, which we might call the 'dream-time' of the Brangwens, covertly enlists Freud's help in effectively playing off our two great primary epics against each other. The Genesis narrative, unlike Homer's as Auerbach tells us at length,[9] is 'fraught with background', 'layered', in other words, and its times and its places are neither measured by the clock nor discoverable upon the map. Both are imbued with significance by the idea of 'waiting upon God', and the Brangwen men, unconsciously steeped in religion, orientate themselves by the Church spire. Past, present, and future are superimposed in an effect of prehistoric timelessness. The 'classlessness' of Scripture, another interesting point of contrast with Homer, resides in the fact that God's will may disclose itself at any moment through anyone, even the most humble, and that *every* life is precious to God, and therefore has its own identifiable plots and themes. Lawrence's myth of origins is saturated in Scripture partly for these reasons, and partly because the Brangwens (i.e. the 'tribe' before it separated out into 'individuals', and for generations thereafter) lived by the Bible. Nevertheless this ritual beginning *is*, of course, a myth of an Eden where language is gesture (imprinted with bodily rhythms) and the World is the World. Expulsion from this unfallen world of faith into the world of fiction (where the World itself is a construct, and the World only brushes the surface of it) stems from the dissatisfaction of 'the women', looking out (as they do in so much Victorian fiction) from the confines of the domestic scene, longingly, passionately, or angrily. As Scripture tells us, therefore, it is through the female that historical time is born (i.e. via mortality). This 'Fall', of course, as Scripture also tells us, is what makes redemption (i.e. the end of time) possible.

It is striking, therefore, that from the moment when the Brangwen women look outwards to the Homeric epic of the aristocrats and landowners, it is they who are the 'consciousness-bearers':

> The male part of the poem was filled in by such men as the vicar and Lord William, lean, eager men with strange movements, men who had command of the further fields, whose lives ranged over a great extent. Ah, it was something very desirable to know, this touch of the wonderful men who had the power of thought and comprehension. The women of the village might be much fonder of Tom Brangwen, and more at their ease with him, yet if their lives had been robbed of the vicar, and of Lord William, the leading shoot would have been cut away from them, they would have been heavy and uninspired and inclined to hate. So long as the wonder of the beyond was before them, they could get along, whatever their lot. And Mrs. Hardy, and the vicar, and Lord William, these moved in the wonder of the beyond, and wcre visible to the eyes of Cossethay in their motion.[10]

It is through the women, restless in their limited traditional roles, that we enter irrevocably into what Lawrence calls 'the spoken world'. To borrow the terminology of the *Study of Thomas Hardy*, which is, as we have seen, the 'metaphysical' text which accompanies *The Rainbow* as *The Crown* accompanies *Women in Love*, the will to inertia (the 'female' principle which the men experience as a 'stabilising' presence in their lives) is countered by the male 'will to motion', though this drama of wills no longer coincides altogether with culturally determined gender roles. The women soon, in the course of this 'overture' to Lawrence's Wagnerian music-drama, become 'the woman', singular and probing. The long, diffuse, unanswerable questions of the first few pages – the patriarchal mode of scripture – give way to the brightly lit Homeric world of travel, discovery, and social intercourse; a world in which *dialogue*, heteroglossia, supplants the monologic Scriptural word.

The courtship of Tom and Lydia already makes apparent the ways in which 'experience' is becoming an issue for a society that has entered historical time and encountered 'otherness'. Lydia, in that chapter with the fairy-tale title ('How Tom Brangwen married a Polish lady') is initially cast in the role of passive recollection, as if she were waiting to be brought back to life (the Sleeping Beauty theme of many of Lawrence's stories). We are still half in the 'dream-time', even if Frieda's quite specific memories of the von Richthofen estates in Prussia supplied much of the 'exotic' information. Tom's courtship (amid stormy Romantic imagery of spring) releases Lydia from her melancholia and her reveries:

> There was a light streaming on to the bushes at the back from the kitchen window. He began to hesitate. How could he do this? Looking through the window, he saw her seated in the rocking-chair with the child, already in its nightdress, sitting on her knee. The fair head with its wild, fierce, hair was drooping towards the fire-warmth, which reflected on the bright cheeks and the clear skin of the child, who seemed to be musing, almost like a grown-up person. The mother's face was dark and still and he saw, with a pang, that she was away back in the life that had been. The child's hair gleamed like spun glass, her face was illuminated till it seemed like wax lit up from the inside. The wind boomed strongly. Mother and child sat motionless, silent, the child staring with vacant dark eyes into the fire, the mother looking into space. The little girl was almost asleep. It was her will which kept her eyes so wide.[11]

Her marriage to Tom unites them both in a bond which is stronger than any merely 'personal' relationship can be, a bond validated by the community, and with a religious reverence for 'otherness'. Lawrence, with his first-hand understanding of what it means to pass through profound spiritual devastation and emerge strengthened, constructs his account of Lydia's sense of alienation in England, the numbness following her husband's death in this 'aloof' foreign country, her retreat into herself and resistance to encroachment from the world until the rather improbable Tom appears, out of Lawrence's own experience of bereavement (his mother's death, evoked in *Sons and Lovers*) and Frieda's experiences too. This latter he does with great tact, making good his claim that in our time work, especially creative work, must be made more the joint task of man and woman. Lawrence and Frieda, at that time, at any rate, could, like Tom and Lydia, give each other space as well as mutual support. Theirs is the rainbow arch that shifts momentarily out of alignment under the pressure of the 'difference' that also constitutes their mutual attraction. But even here, east of Eden, the pillar of cloud by day and the pillar of fire by night weave together in a pledge of the everlasting sanctity of marriage, which in turn constitutes the strongest evidence of the reality of the transcendental.

This, in turn, sustains the next generation. The gentle wry humour of Chapter Five, 'The Wedding at the Marsh', which helps to ease Anna and Will's difficult rite of passage, owes much to Tom's sense of being, deep down, at peace with himself. His fatuous, slightly tipsy, metaphysics, are altogether in place, and deeply reassuring:

> '*If* we've got to be Angels,' went on Tom Brangwen, haranguing the company at large, 'and if there is no such thing as a man nor a woman amongst them, then it seems to me as a married couple makes one Angel.'
>
> 'It's the brandy,' said Alfred Brangwen wearily.
>
> 'For,' said Tom Brangwen, and the company was listening to the conundrum, 'an Angel can't be *less* than a human being. And if it was only the soul of a man *minus* the man, then it would be less than a human being.'
>
> 'Decidedly,' said Alfred.
>
> And a laugh went round the table. But Tom Brangwen was inspired.[12]

Anna, as a child, is sustained and supported by the strength of Tom and Lydia's relationship, which never loses altogether the aura of myth, and is itself underpinned by tradition, folklore, and (above all) patriarchy. The great bow of the overarching narrative, threatening as well as promising and protective, working through a rhythm of repetition, dissolution, and renewal, aligns Tom and Lydia with Noah and with the portentous arch set in the heavens after the Flood.

For Lydia's daughter Anna, however, as she grows up, the world takes on a different 'look': it delivers a challenge she must rise to (and it is significant, after all, that Tom is not her father). Her difference is apparent in her girlhood, but it grows upon her when she encounters mature experience. She is not, of course, alone; the gathering of the sheaves which forms the centrepiece of her courtship of Will is controlled by the double rhythm of work and desire, opposites reconciled as if the two had never been culturally sundered. Yet from the outset there is also strife, born of the different expectations of male and female, and consequent especially upon that crossing-over of the 'will to motion' and the 'will to inertia' (cf. the *Study of Thomas Hardy*, examined later in this chapter). Their honeymoon reworks (or 'deconstructs') the Genesis theme of Noah's Ark by giving Anna the power to overturn the Mosaic codes and send Will's tablets of the Law crashing down the hillside; a shock to him, like all the other intrusions of the female into his rapt, self-obsessed male world. A more ominous sequence is the one in which she mocks at, and is instrumental in destroying, his carving of Adam and Eve; she derides the Biblical iconography of Eve being born from Adam's rib in defiance of the 'natural' order of things.

'Why don't you go on with your woodcarving?' she said. 'Why don't you finish your Adam and Eve?'

But she did not care for the Adam and Eve, and he never put another stroke to it. She jeered at the Eve, saying 'She is like a little marionette. Why is she so small? You've made Adam as big as God, and Eve like a doll.'

'It is impudence to say that Woman was made out of Man's body,' she continued, 'when every man is born of woman. What impudence men have, what arrogance!'

In a rage one day, after trying to work on the board, and failing, so that his belly was a flame of nausea, he chopped up the

whole panel and put it on the fire. She did not know. He went
about for some days very quiet and subdued after it.

'Where is the Adam and Eve board?' she asked him.

She looked at him.

'But your carving.'

'I burned it.'

'When?'

She did not believe him.

'When I was at the March?'

'Yes.'

She said no more.[13]

Anna affirms her female self-sufficiency again during the episode where she dances naked to herself, appropriating the Scriptural paradigm of Saul and David (maybe Salome, too), excluding the
male, or perhaps even, like Salome, the favourite *femme fatale* of the
decadence, covertly demanding the head of her husband (the
prophet) upon a platter.[14] In her pregnancy she requires no more
from him. Will's resolve, which, despite his stubbornness, was
always a shaky thing, is broken by these reiterated assaults, and his
attempt to recover a sense of his potency (building assertively up to,
but characteristically not following through, the seduction of a
working girl in Nottingham) leaves him frustrated and with an
exacerbated sense of the potential destructiveness of his own
sexuality. In these overheated pages Lawrence invokes the 'decadent' iconography we have already encountered, with reference to
the *fin-de-siècle*, in *The White Peacock*; but in this novel it is all much
more sharply in focus and unerringly appropriate, even to the
extent of Lawrence boldly aligning Will with Jack the Ripper as he
'enjoys' Anna's body piecemeal, desperate as he is to repossess the
irreplaceable fulfilled 'experience' which he knows is draining out
of his world:

> This was what their love had become, a sensuality violent and
> extreme as death. They had no conscious intimacy, no tender-
> ness of love. It was all the lust and the infinite maddening
> intoxication of the senses, a passion of death.[15]

There can be no doubt that the violently hostile reactions to *The
Rainbow* when it first appeared, as well as being engineered by the

Home Office, as Harry T. Moore tells us, had not a little to do with Lawrence's temerity in presuming to bring together the 'under-world' of sexual desire (the Victorians' guilty secrets) and the sacrosanct institution of marriage. Something is, of course, going wrong between Anna and Will, but in the wider circle of things both are seen as victims of an accelerating process of which the 1870 Education Act is at once both symptom and cause, a progressive loss of spiritual bearings in an increasingly mechanised society. Will's destruction of his carving is, among other things, a capitulation to this process. He takes refuge in 'the new Swedish methods' (I suppose Lawrence means to suggest something rather passionless), loses himself in teaching woodwork, and turns away from the unresolved, unresolvable problems of his marriage, while Anna, for her part, is content to let others continue, on her behalf, the Pilgrim's Progress towards the end of the rainbow/end of *The Rainbow*.

With Will and Anna, we are made sharply aware of the fact that conventional moral judgements about the 'success' or 'failure' of a relationship are largely irrelevant; a refinement of Nietzsche's 'amoralism' is a crucial dimension of Lawrence's arguments about the absence of the 'old stable ego' in his novel. His implicit thesis at this point is that a change in sensibility has come about in late Victorian England (i.e. the period in which he became a teenager), although those who are undergoing this change cannot properly articulate it. It is significant that the iconography of the Gothic Revival, with its rather febrile attempts to respiritualise an increasingly mechanical mass civilisation, has left its impress on the parts of the novel dealing with this generation. Will's interest in ecclesiastical art, for instance, as in the reiterated motif of the round and broken arches, and the stained glass which Victorian artists revived, are just a part of the Ruskin/Morris inspired movement that culminated in Arts and Crafts and Art Nouveau, the predecessors of the Modernist aesthetic in which this novel is steeped. This late Romantic art is poignant with loss and defeat. Will has certainly been 'cheated out of his experience', though it would be hard to say exactly by whom; if Anna had been cheated too, this may well be because she could not be fulfilled while he was not, since her marriage was, when all was said and done, at the heart of her 'experience' of life, even to the exclusion of other necessary things.

For their daughter Ursula, courtship and marriage lack any special kind of inevitability. For one thing, the patriarchal myth, which held these values in place, is dead (though, of course, it refuses to lie down, especially in the shape of those who, like Skrebensky, use the imperial war machine as a camouflage for their own personal emptiness). In a remarkable piece of Modernist textual counterpoint[16] Ursula mockingly quotes a substantial passage from Genesis on rainbows and floods, juxtaposing this brazenly patriarchal monologue with some fragments of (polytheistic) Greek myth, so that, by a play of ironies, one fiction appears to be no more or less 'true' than another.

'And I will remember my covenant, which is between me and you and every living creature of all flesh, and the waters shall no more become a flood to destroy all flesh.' 'Destroy all flesh', why 'flesh' in particular? Who was this lord of flesh? After all, how big was the Flood? Perhaps a few dryads and fauns had just run into the hills and the further valleys and woods, frightened, but most had gone on blithely unaware of any flood at all, unless the nymphs should tell them. It pleased Ursula to think of the naiads in Asia Minor meeting the nereids at the mouth of the streams, where the sea washed against the fresh, sweet tide, and calling to their sisters the news of Noah's Flood.[17]

In this way Lawrence's novel enters into a dialogue with its own sub-text and is made to interrogate its own ideology and the systems of values underlying its themes and variations and *Leitmotiven.*

Instrumental to this process, Ursula tries out, in the course of her adolescence, a variety of literary and painterly stereotypes of femininity ('in her bedroom window with her black, rough hair on her shoulders, and her warm face all rapt').[18] She also gives expression to her passionate Romantic idealism, and reacts sharply against Skrebensky by embarking upon a love affair with one of her schoolteachers, Winifred Inger (the title of the chapter that describes this, 'Shame', must surely, like many chapter titles in *Women in Love,* be understood as being in parentheses). This is a relationship designed to exclude men, but in the end she is unable to sustain it and commit herself totally to her lover. For Ursula, this passionate experience is more like a 'Hellenic' retreat from the gritty male 'Hebraism' that surrounds her (to make an apposite application of Arnold's influential terms in *Culture and Anarchy*)[19] than a statement of freely contracted political and sexual commitment.

Education looks to Ursula like the natural way out of an emotional impasse, as it was for her father, for Lawrence, and for many more people than would perhaps wish to admit it; and with the passing of the 1870 Education Act, and the greatly increased demand for teachers, it seems for a while that a career in teaching will supply Ursula with a viable identity which she can use to challenge the patriarchal order on its own ground. In point of fact the struggle (and we are painfully aware of Lawrence writing out of his own sensitive 'female' self, and the bitter struggle of his tough Croydon years) was too harsh. Ursula's crisis (breakdown and miscarriage) follows the climax of destructiveness that ends her relationship with the 'burning and corroding' Skrebensky. Her battle is largely with herself, as the fact of the miscarriage possibly symbolises; at all events her assault on the 'embryonic' fish-like boy William hurts her, in the time-honoured school phrase, more than it hurts him. Even her final 'New Testament' vision of the rainbow, Blake-like and apocalyptic, is a *personal* reaffirmation of a tentative faith in what is no longer God's great unshakeable arch.

> And the rainbow stood on the earth. She knew that the sordid people who crept hard-scaled and separate on the face of the world's corruption were living still, that the rainbow was arched in their blood and would quiver to life in their spirit, that they would cast off their horny covering of disintegration, that new, clean, naked bodies would issue to a new germination, to a new growth, rising to the light and the wind and the clean rain of heaven. She saw in the rainbow the earth's new architecture, the old, brittle corruption of houses and factories swept away, the world built up in a living fabric of Truth, fitting to the overarching heavens.[20]

From some angles, *The Rainbow* looks like an exercise in the Victorian 'higher criticism'. The Yeatsian propositions that 'things fall apart' and that 'the centre cannot hold' fit it, in some respects, very well, and as the gyres turn (Yeats's view of historical process is very like Lawrence's) 'the falcon cannot hear the falconer'.[21] Only, as Lawrence himself said, the 'rhythm' of his novel is 'destructive-consummating', so that where Yeats imagines some strange beast 'shuffling towards Bethlehem', Lawrence, like Eliot, finds renewal and a tentative kind of hope in the processes of disintegration. Nevertheless, the transition from the Age of Law to the Age of Love (with an ominous pre-echo of Orwell's Ministry of Love) that *The Rainbow* enacts, follows the metaphysics of Lawrence's *Hardy* study already referred to, where Lawrence, after a Nietzschean preamble establishing art's 'gratuitousness', develops his thesis, which I have commented upon in passing, about the polarisation of male and female as the dynamic principle at work in the formation of culture. An argument about the internal self-divisions of our age, analogous to Eliot's thesis about the 'dissociation of sensibility' that 'set in' in the seventeenth century ('The Metaphysical Poets', 1918), Lawrence's synchronic and diachronic model of the inter-relations of the 'will to motion' and the 'will to inertia' differs from Eliot's account of dissociation in that there is no suggestion in Lawrence that there ever was, or could be, an 'ultimate' state of balanced integration, only, as in the Futurism that attracted him (and which has left a deep imprint on *Women in Love*), a changing and complex tension of opposites.

When the Age of Law began to give way, at the Renaissance, to the Age of Love (these terms, loose as they seem, *can* be given a content), the long crucifixion of Flesh by Spirit was set under way, a dubious 'freedom' being thus won with great pain from the martyrdom of the body. One can indeed say, without much exaggeration, that this is Hardy's main theme. Christianity may (among other things) be held accountable for the perpetuation of this self-division (and Lawrence liked to quote Swinburne's 'Thou hast conquered, O pale Galilean'): but Victorian agnosticism, as Hardy clearly shows us, is the immediate source of the death-agony and the torment of the modern spirit. Hardy's characters are 'crucified' by the persistence of a faith in which they no longer believe. As it survives in the conduct of Sue and Jude, for example, it is largely destructive, while as the basis of the conventional social morality that condemns them it is horrifyingly repressive. The battle between flesh and spirit, law and love, each unable to 'connect', is what agitates the modern world and comprises our reality. Thus the 'will-to-motion' (male, spiritual) is like a wheel turning upon the axle (Lawrence says 'hub', but no matter) of the 'will to inertia' (female, fleshly) in a constant exchange of energies. The whole process is much more complex (and less sexist) than this suggests, since the 'rim' of the wheel could not articulate its movement without its point of stasis, and the axle is what actually moves forward (the wheel just goes round and round). The 'wills' in question are actually the opposite of what they appear to be (trust Lawrence to reinvent the wheel).

If all this sounds very complicated and self-contradictory, these contradictions are indeed actively present in Hardy's novels, especially in *Jude* (see, for instance, Jude's conflicting drives towards Sue and Arabella, and the hopeless confusion that sets each at cross-purposes with the others because they are all demanding something that at any given moment the object of desire is incapable of reciprocating). Still, it should be said that Lawrence's novel has moved, in important respects, far beyond the rather doctrinaire terms of Victorian cultural criticism and the heavy hand of agnosticism. For one thing, it is the disappearance of 'the falconer', in the guise of the omniscient narrator, that makes possible the continuous subtle shifts of narrative distance by means of which Lawrence traces the endless 'becoming' of his 'unstable egos'. In another section of the letter to Garnett quoted earlier, he speaks of his characters falling into a kind of rhythmic pattern (rather than the linear action of the novel developing in relation to an equally linear development of characters). The analogy he offers, which I explore in relation to the structure of *Women in Love* (where it is more clearly demonstrable), is the experiment in physics known as Chladni's Plate, wherein a thin metal plate is scattered with fine sand grains and then set vibrating by the experimenter drawing a violin bow down its edge; whereupon, as Lawrence has it, 'the sand takes lines unknown'.[22] The narrator's random and unrecorded interventions generate around themselves an 'aura' of meaning analogous to the 'luminous halo' invoked in Virginia Woolf's essay on modern fiction.[23] The heyday of Modernism is, as all commentators agree, a period of unprecedented symbiosis in the arts; writing and unwriting space is the novelistic equivalent of the Impressionist undertaking to paint time; and Lawrence was caught up in this process more completely than most, being unusually responsive to the visual arts.

While he was writing the novel in Italy in 1913 and 1914, Lawrence came upon the work of the Italian Futurists, and his imagination was fired by the technique of what these artists themselves described as 'simultaneity' in (for instance) Boccioni's *Development of a Bottle through Space*, which Lawrence comments on in the Hardy study. The analytical representation of 'the lines of force which create the state of rest called a bottle' in Boccioni's sculpture insists, says Lawrence, on the 'male spirit of motion outwards' as a response to the Italian stasis of three centuries and the preponderance of the female in a largely matriarchal culture (interesting comparisons and contrasts with English society become possible). Art historians agree about the very specific social and economic forces that generated Futurism as a phenomenon specific to Italian society, which was industrialising and urbanising very rapidly; and what he saw of this gave a new impetus to Lawrence's complex vision of industrialism, formed by English Romanticism but conceived in the shadow of the pits. The simultaneous movement outwards and inwards of the Boccioni sculpture and other Futurist works, the artists' fascination with exploring the properties of the material, and the dynamism and tension of the sculpted artistic space (Lawrence's favourite notion of 'relatedness'), representing (for example) a bottle as it 'emerges' within the space it occupies and gradually takes on shape, form and function under the active gaze of the beholder, fascinated Lawrence. In part Boccioni's bottle self-evidently derives from the Impressionist art object, which exists in an open-ended moment of time as an effect of light. It is therefore, like the Impressionist canvas, a phenomenological proposition, i.e. the thing itself is not distinct from the act of perceiving it. More demonstratively than Impressionism, however, it is situated within the space which it occupies and structures (Boccioni inherited the Italian 'public' tradition of sculpture), and in this space it generates dialogue energised by the tensions of surface and depth which it sets up.

Lawrence could see Italian Futurist art as essentially argumentative or polemical, like his own work, and Utopian in a way he thought he understood. But it is also a proposition about existence, laying bare the 'existential' ground of being in a modern, technological idiom. Marinetti has a fondness for the term 'scomposizione', sometimes unfortunately translated as 'decomposition': 'deconstruction' would be more precise. What he means by this is that in any creative process analysis and synthesis take place simultaneously; there is no such thing as a 'complete' work of art, but for reasons slightly different from those given by the Impressionists. In Futurist aesthetics, every work of art is caught up in a nexus of dialogues with its historical moment, its materials, its environment, and its reception. In *The Rainbow*, people, things, landscapes, and abstractions interpenetrate in changing patterns of 'relatedness' like Boccioni's 'lines of force'. They disclose their 'futurity' by their openness to still latent and undisclosed meanings (some vividly evoke a Lawrencian mood of prophecy). If, as I have suggested, the Utopian element in Futurism struck a chord in Lawrence, it should be added that he did *not* share the admiration for Fascism which some of the Futurists saw as the logical political step forward from their fascination with masculinity, hardness, and impersonality. But the open-ended dialogue between form and substance, matter and metaphysic, technology and the human subject, art object and environment – all dimensions of the Futurist 'fields of force'[24] – are built into *The Rainbow* in differential proportion to the disintegration of the patriarchal Old Testament paradigm. It remains therefore to look at the textures and structures of Lawrence's writing in a little more detail in order to substantiate these claims.

In a pioneering stylistic essay entitled 'The Narrative Technique of the Rainbow',[25] Roger Sale comments on Lawrence's peculiar sense of space/time, and the syntax which organises it:

> In establishing a causal 'when he, then she' relationship, Lawrence breaks down the specific time and replaces it with a tight unity of the two figures at a general time. . . . In the next short paragraph all time and space are missing: "Very good, she was the enemy, very good. As he prowled round her, she watched him. As he struck at her, she struck back."[26]

Roger Fowler has noted in a similar context the 's/he' which is partly an 'I', peculiar to Lawrence's narrative. Such devices spatialise narrative time by releasing it from the sequentiality of chronometric cause and effect; they also release characters from the constraints of an 'individuality' or 'stable ego' constructed from a determinate narrative point of view, and present them as 'emergent', in the Futurist way. Sale concludes:

> Thus, in less than a page, we move from an action unspecified in time and space, to one in which time and space are ambivalent, to

one in which they do not exist, to one in which they are very much present, and back again to one where they are unspecified. We learn not only about particular events, but also about a world in which there is nothing but Will and Anna.[27]

Sale wants to push on to a value-judgement; such a relationship, he tells us, is bound to 'fail'. Lawrence's emphasis, as we have already seen, is subtly but crucially different. Anna and Will have become caught, through some inner capitulation, but more or less despite themselves, in Yeats' ominous gyre wherein 'the falcon cannot hear the falconer', where the signifier is split from, and in pursuit of, the signified (compare, and contrast, the gathering of the sheaves). Will, child of the law and wedded to the monologic Truth of his cathedral and its cultural transpositions (Gothic art and its nineteenth-century derivative) is ill-equipped to enter this 'Futurist' world, our world, in which every position, every relationship, is fissured with relativism and calls for a constant succession of existential 'leaps' and bold improvisations (cf. *Women in Love*). The mainstay of Lawrence's style here, and perhaps everywhere else, is repetition, which he once justified in a loosely sexual metaphor as enacting a pulsing to-and-fro rhythm rising to a climax.[28] In point of fact, the slight changes of angle noted by Sale, superimposed one on top of another like Boccioni's 'lines of force', trace the contours of thought and feeling in the process of formation:

> She was afraid of his hard, evil movements, the head dropped a little rigidly, in a crouching, cruel way. She was afraid of him. He seemed to lacerate her sensitive femaleness. He seemed to hurt her womb, to take pleasure in torturing her.[29]

The tension of opposites here, and the 'dynamic' expression, on the surface of the writing, in the imagery, of an inner force thrusting through to expression, is Futuristic; so, perhaps, is the sexism. Or again:

> Suddenly his heart was torn with compassion for her. He became alive again, in an anguish of compassion. He could not bear to think of her tears – he could not bear it. He wanted to go to her and pour out his heart's blood to her. He wanted to give everything to her, all his blood, his life, to the last dregs, pour

everything away to her. He yearned with passionate desire to offer himself to her, utterly.[30]

The repetitions, like the 'gyres' of Boccioni's bottle, build up an intensity and density of experience, where once again depth meets surface in a series of charged gestures. Where Proust or James gather up the threads of consciousness, with whatever difficulty, into a continuum, and authenticate their worlds subjectively, Lawrence fills the gap left by waning experience differently, spatialising time (in the Futuristic or Cubist way) in terms of sets of simultaneous planes interacting to form a composite expressive image of relatedness. There is no 'subject' in the old sense, so there can be no continuity of subjectivity, still less a stream of conscious-ness of the Woolf or Joyce kind. The repetitions always have an air of improvisation and unfinishedness, being subject to interruption (also intrinsic to Futurism): the last word has never been said, as with Birkin's *Lebensphilosophie* in *Women in Love*. Much misleading criticism of Lawrence is a consequence of nailing the author down, erroneously, to the provisional and hypothetical positions he has taken up heuristically and in relation to the changing emotional and spiritual forms of his characters' lives. As in life, so in his novels, people feel differently, act differently, at different times.

All of this accelerating psycho-drama is wrongly perceived by Sale as a growing loss of control on Lawrence's part. In the courtship of Ursula and Skrebensky

> There is an attempt to return to the novel's original terms . . . But even in the scene in which they make love in the stackyard, which echoes the sheaves-gathering scene with Will and Anna, some-thing is out of control.[31]

Things get worse, he claims:

> And timorously, his hand went over her, over the salt, compact brilliance of her body. If he could but have her, how he would enjoy her! If he could but net her brilliant, cold, salt-burning body in the soft iron of his own hands, net her, capture her, hold her down, how madly he would enjoy her. He strove subtly but with all his energy, to enclose her, to have her. And always she was burning and brilliant and hard as salt, and deadly. Yet

obstinately, all his flesh burning and corroding, as if he were invaded by some consuming, scathing poison, he still persisted, thinking at last he might overcome her. Even, in his frenzy, he sought for her mouth, though it was like putting his face into some awful death. She yielded to him, and he pressed himself upon her in extremity, his soul groaning over and over.[32]

('It is a blessing', says Sale, that the following line, 'Let me come – let me come' had to be cut from the text of the first edition.) Curious how a perceptive modern commentator can still be offended by the more extreme expressions of sexual passion in Lawrence, even when the novelist is being exceptionally true to the kind of experience he is describing. 'Let me come' is, on one level, an altogether comprehensible plea in an age when contraceptives were little used; on another, it expresses admirably Skrebensky's hopeless striving for release from emotional torment. In any case, to talk of 'loss of control' on anyone's part but Skrebensky's is really beside the point. This startlingly original appropriation of the inorganic, quasi-scientific imagery of Futurism half-conceals the story of Lot's wife (Ursula is referred to specifically as a 'pillar of salt' a few pages earlier, and Lawrence in a poem, and elsewhere, rather harshly applied the image to Frieda *vis-à-vis* her children). In *Genesis*, Lot is one of the legendary ancestors, nephew to Abraham. His 'promised land' was the site of the cities of Sodom and Gomorrah (Lawrence's scenario is being played out in a decadent era of growing military and imperial menace). In a story not unlike that of Orpheus and Euridice, Lot and his daughters are turned away from the cities by an angel, but his wife, looking back – i.e. defying patriarchal authority – was changed into a pillar of salt. The double-voiced narrative in this passage, situated on the interface between the consciousness of the two protagonists, is thus given a crucial additional voicing in terms of the 'unweaving' of the Genesis rainbow. Can one really imagine Ursula mixing the gin and tonic for the other officers' wives? The act of transgression, the frantic demand for the absolute, is arrested by her nets, salt, iron, and poison. One might be forgiven for thinking that the 'ego' had fragmented beyond repair. But the corrosive salt is also a purifying agent; every 'scomposizione' is a potentially creative act of renewal. For Ursula's generation it is no longer possible, and perhaps no longer necessary, to take refuge from the 'corrosiveness' of frustration and misery in some kind of displacement activity, as Will and Anna do. Ursula will battle through on her own account, uncompromisingly, and find a man who is not emotionally dependent, like Skrebensky, nor, like him, a hollow careerist. Of course, there is a price to be paid: her deep depression, or breakdown. But she does recover. The proper riposte to Sale lies in the comments offered above as well as Lawrence's own words:

> The novel is a perfect medium for revealing to us the changing rainbow of our living relationships. The novel can help us to live as nothing else can; no didactic Scripture, anyhow.[33]

I like to think that this was what Bakhtin meant, too, when he wrote that

> The novelistic word registers with extreme subtlety the tiniest shifts and oscillations of the social atmosphere; it does so, moreover, while registering it as a whole, in all its aspects.[34]

Here, or hereabouts, is the 'dialogic principle'.

4
'The effects of the War'
Women in Love

As I have suggested, the famous letter ('stable ego') is even more illuminating with respect to *Women in Love* than it is in relation to *The Rainbow*. The figure of Chladni's Plate is highly appropriate to Lawrence's way of organising the later novel, in that the 'experimental' method of the plate allows the author to efface himself as systematically as Joyce does in *Ulysses* (though with similarly equivocal results, since there are more and less histrionic ways of making one's exit). Chladni's metal plate both is, and is not, like the photographic plate (which was originally made of metal coated with chemicals) since it is a two-dimensional surface which receives a 'message' that contains both depth and resonance. The 'image' formed upon it, which is never 'fixed' (unlike the photograph) is a sensitive vehicle for registering invisible sound waves rather than light waves, and it responds to the vibrations set up by the violin bow, a kind of silent 'Dionysiac' music, which is given a provisional 'Apollonian' shape. The 'constellation' (to borrow Mallarmé's word) of its shape depends upon random factors, like the French poet's famous throw of the dice (his analogy for the set of relations between the creative process and the 'finished' work, which actually never *is* finished).[1]

Unlike the photographic plate, where the image cannot change once the processing has taken place, Chladni's Plate keeps the image in a state of suspended 'becoming' since even a slight shift in the position of the fiddle-bow is enough for the sand patterns to take on a quite different internal organisation. Lawrence does not say so in so many words, but there is no doubt that the 'Chladni's Plate' thesis is a contribution to the vexed (and largely inept) debate about photography and representationalism in the early modern period. Characters, ideas, *objets d'art*, even linguistic topoi fall into kaleidoscopic patterns in response to a powerful intervention, or set of interventions, in the fictional world from what seems, in the degree of its disengagement, more like the cine camera than the authorial pen; the angle of intervention is crucial, but cannot be pinned down to a human agent. In response to this intervention Futurist 'lines of force', fissuring the surface of the narrative, generate proliferating and sometimes almost random sets of relationships and tensions between people and objects, images and symbols. It does not surprise us to find David Lodge describing the plot of this novel as 'tenuous', since it is scarcely even a 'plot of ideas' and the short, discrete, imagistic chapters operate by starting up chain reactions in characters and situations which in turn generate another set of images. Lawrence himself spoke of the 'purely destructive' rhythm of his novel (as opposed to *The Rainbow*, which was 'destructive-consummating'), and he ascribed this to the War, the effects of which, he said, were to be felt in the characters (even though the First World War itself is hardly mentioned; Russell's film combined some forceful images of war with costumes which were mostly, at least for the women – which could be part of the point – post-war).[2] In point of fact, a more appropriate word than Lawrence's 'destructive' might be 'deconstructive'. The chapters of the novel can be described as 'diagrammatic' because they generate an intricate discourse around an object, or an art object, which serves as a focal point for a kind of conceptual debate and an open-ended play of images: this device finds its most explicit thematisation in the 'School-room' chapter.

The novel begins and ends in mid-conversation, and there is an overall effect of a lot of loose ends and unfinished business, especially in the relationship of Birkin and Hermione (but in this pairing, and in others, the characters suffer from a kind of repetition compulsion, which gives an 'organisation' of a sort). And yet, paradoxically, there is a strenuous, even strident, exchange of well-defined views about the world going on through all of this. Maybe people are talking for their lives: for when the talk ceases, it gives way to an ominous 'dumb show' in which an improvisation around a cluster of key issues – half-way between charade and psychodrama – comes to the verge of giving cathartic expression to some urgent issue, only to break off with a characteristic 'interrupted' or 'frozen' gesture. If there is a forward movement, it is

rather like that in T. S. Eliot's 'The Waste Land', which this novel
strongly resembles both in its surface organisation and in its
underlying assumptions about civilisation and its discontents; there
is a kind of painful fitting together, by the author as much as by the
reader, of the pieces of a jigsaw, in the knowledge that the most
important ones are missing and will probably never turn up. In the
chapter called (with a succinctness typical of this novel) 'Rabbit', for
instance, Gudrun goes to Shortlands to teach art to young
Winifred, being half-aware, at the same time, that to do so is
'equivalent to accepting Gerald Crich as a lover', and she under-
standably has very mixed feelings about this (she must know, but
never says, that she and Gerald have little in common except a
craving for fulfilment through extreme sensation, and a kind of
death wish). The undertone of violence and death that runs
through the chapter is sounded initially by an echo of the water-
party sequence and Gudrun's recollections of Winifred. The girl's
behaviour now is a bit jumpy and odd, suggesting insecurity and
reminiscent of the trauma of her 'calling from the steamer in the
night'. The struggle for supremacy between Gudrun and Gerald is
prefigured by the almost predatory designs the former has on the
dog, Looloo: '"Let us draw Looloo,' said Gudrun, 'and see if we can
get his Looliness, shall we?"' We are back in the world of penis-
envy, or the castration complex, or both. Unsurprisingly, the
'chagrined little dog' turns out, in her picture, as 'a grotesque little
diagram of a grotesque little animal'. When Gerald appears he
seems, on the face of it, in good shape, but at the same time he has
'a fear about him, as of something wanting'. Clearly he is the next
in line to get 'done', after Looloo and Bismarck (splendid combina-
tion of names). Winifred, a perceptive child, has an intuition of
what is going on, and it is she who 'sets up' the rabbit as a symbolic
agent of wrath (Bismarck is 'fierce' and 'splendid'). The multilingual conversation that follows, redolent of the heteroglossia of 'The
Waste Land',[3] skims eerily over the surface of the psychic traumas
of war; reiterated words are 'Wünder', 'mystère', 'König', 'chance-
lier', a sort of hypnotic rhapsody of power, the struggle for power
in Europe but also the power game that is under way between
Gudrun and Gerald. Finally, as Gerald says, by way of commentary, Bismarck, the chancellor, is a sort of 'judge'; and this is truer
than he knows, because the apparently harmless but actually
vicious (because frightened) rabbit cathects the violence of Gerald

and Gudrun's relationship and reflects it back, magnified, hyperbolic, as an 'effect of the War': also the modern war of the sexes, long contained, if not suppressed, by the hypocrisies attendant upon Victorian patriarchy:

> The long, demon-like beast lashed out again, spread on the air as if it were flying, looking something like a dragon, then closing up again, inconceivably powerful and explosive. The man's body, strung to its efforts, vibrated strongly. Then a sudden sharp, white-edged wrath came up in him. Swift as lightning he drew back and brought his free hand down like a hawk on the neck of the rabbit. Simultaneously, there came the unearthly abhorrent scream of a rabbit in the fear of death. It made one immense writhe, tore his wrists and his sleeves in a final convulsion, all its belly flashed white in a whirlwind of paws, and then he had slung it round and had it under his arm fast. It cowered and skulked. His face was gleaming with a smile. "You wouldn't think that there was all that force in a rabbit," he said, looking at Gudrun. And he saw her eyes black as night in her pallid face, she looked almost unearthly. The scream of the rabbit, after the violent tussle, seemed to have torn the veil of her consciousness. He looked at her, and the whitish, electric gleam in his face intensified.

Gudrun's rage against the 'dumb' creature is clearly a kind of projection; glancing at Gerald 'she revealed again the mocking, white-cruel recognition. There was a league between them abhorrent to them both. They were implicated with each other in abhorrent mysteries.' The insistent process of projection and over-determination affects the language, turbid and veering out of control, characteristically situated somewhere in between the narrator and the character, a language which is specific to the emotional tensions in the situation as well as redolent of war. Blood has been shed on both sides; her 'deep red score', 'long shallow red rip' is like a wound in his brain (bringing in again, as if from the early *Trespasser*, the Oedipal fear of castration). And the rabbit suddenly gyrates 'as if shot from a gun'. Winifred pronounces the sinister-elegaic-erotic epilogue; '"Let its mother stroke its fur then, darling, because it is so mysterious."' It sure is: it is pure id.

The similarities between this chapter and parts of 'The Waste

Land' are not fortuitous. Although Lawrence's novel was written in
the midst of the experience of war, it was published in England at
almost the same moment as Eliot's great poem of breakdown, and it
is already asking the 'postwar' questions ('What are the roots that
clutch/Out of this stony rubbish?'). Both works are haunted by the
unburied dead; not just the victims of war (like the crippled Sir
Clifford in *Lady Chatterley's Lover* or Eliot's 'Marie' and the other
'displaced persons' that wars throw up), but the ghosts haunting a
whole culture which has 'exploded', like Tennyson's Kraken, when
war has forced it to the surface and brought it face to face with its
carefully hidden hypocrisies and evasions.[4] At the very beginning
of Lawrence's novel, as in the first lines of Eliot's poem, a low-key
'tracking' shot evokes a prolonged mood of disconsolate waiting
and irresolution (beautifully rendered in Ken Russell's film) and
introduces the 'displaced' sisters, Gudrun and Ursula, who are
trying hard to imagine a future for themselves in the limited
conventional ways available. The argument is inevitably conducted
in terms of 'experience', that elusive entity which for the moment
seems to turn upon 'good offers' – of marriage, of course, in the
absence of any real alternative strategies. Gudrun, the fiercer and
more disenchanted of the two, strikes a note that resonates
throughout the novel, and goes on resonating in Lawrence's work
up to and including *Lady Chatterley's Lover*:

"Don't you find, that things fail to materialise? *Nothing material-
ises!* Everything withers in the bud."
     "What withers in the bud?" asked Ursula.
     "Oh, everything – oneself – things in general." There was a
pause, whilst each sister vaguely considered her fate.
     "It does frighten one," said Ursula, and again there was a
pause. "But do you hope to get anywhere by just marrying?"
     "It seems to be the inevitable next step," said Gudrun.
     Ursula pondered this, with a little bitterness. She was a class
mistress herself, in Willey Green Grammar School, as she had
been for some years.
     "I know," she said, "it seems like that when one thinks in the
abstract. But really imagine it: imagine any man who knows,
imagine him coming home to one every evening, and saying
"Hello", and giving one a kiss –
     There was a blank pause.

"Yes," said Gudrun, in a narrowed voice. "It's just impossible. The man makes it impossible."

"Of course there's children – " said Ursula doubtfully.

Gudrun's face hardened.

"Do you *really* want children, Ursula?" she asked coldly. A dazzled, baffled look came on Ursula's face.

"One feels it is still beyond one," she said.

"*Do* you feel like that?" asked Gudrun. "I get no feeling whatever from the thought of bearing children."

Gudrun looked at Ursula with a mask-like, expressionless face.[5]

From the woman bearing down in labour of 'Totem' to Birkin's final 'I wanted it' the novel proliferates images of maimed and arrested development, depersonalisation, loss of faith in the future, the elusiveness of 'experience'. As the girls continue talking, a persistent note of alienation enters their conversation, registered especially by the grating, off-hand use of the impersonal 'one' instead of the personal pronouns; they become almost as ethereal as Eliot's shadowy but suffering personae, Marie or the typist of the Fire Sermon. Already there is a difference between Ursula and Gudrun, or, to be more precise, the sisters are being defined through their 'relatedness'. With Ursula, there is still the shadowy presence of her recent crisis and rebirth, described in *The Rainbow*: 'in the darkness, something was coming to pass'. Much depends upon her maintaining this openness to experience. With Gudrun, on the other hand, who 'shrank cruelly from this amorphous ugliness of a small colliery town in the Midlands', what matters most is to hang on to her precarious identity as an artist, which she feels to be more or less identical with her identity as a person: attention is drawn to her camouflage of 'grass-green velour hat, her full soft coat of a strong blue colour'.[6] Gudrun's art, which is genuine enough, is a series of perspective games and adroit shifts of focus, radical in its approach to cognitive structures and, like Modernist experimentalism, a vivid way of knowing the world, but, as Lawrence says of Jane Austen, of 'knowing in apartness'. Unsurprisingly, the watery *fleurs du mal*, mud-rooted lilies of the decadence, attract her greatly, and in Chapter Ten, 'Sketch-Book', Gerald and Hermione between them contrive to drop her sketch-book into the muddy element from which these flowers grow, in a kind of battle of wills that leaves Gudrun in no doubt that Gerald is attracted to her: such is the stuff of 'disintegrative' passion:

> What she could see was mud, soft, oozy, watery mud, and from
> its festering chill, water-plants rose up, thick and cool and fleshy,
> very straight and turgid, thrusting out their leaves at right
> angles, and having dark lurid colours, dark green blotches of
> black-purple and bronze. But she could feel their turgid fleshy
> structure as in a sensuous vision, she *knew* how they thrust out
> from themselves, how they stood stiff and succulent against the
> air.[7]

Gudrun also likes to see things 'through the wrong end of a
telescope', as with Looloo. But whatever animus may be expressed
here (the comment about the 'diminishing' vision was probably
prompted by the example of Katherine Mansfield, one source for
the portrait of Gudrun and a practitioner of the 'small' art of the
short story) the attentive reader cannot fail to notice that Lawrence's novel shares with Gudrun's art a certain schematism and a
'diagrammatic' quality, as well as a use of reversed perspective that
locates the source of illumination in a rabbit or a cat and then
projects a diffuse beam outwards from the art object into the
fictional space and beyond into the 'real' world. It may strike us as
odd that Lawrence (and some of his characters) should take against
an art (Gudrun's) that sounds rather like Gaudier-Brzeska's, when
the 'imagistic' technique of the novel itself is directly in line with
similar tendencies that are quite central to Modernism. Yet the
animus against Gudrun also takes its place within the dialectic of
opposites upon which the novel is built.

These opposites are remarkably similar to the dialectic that
shapes the aesthetic philosophy expounded in one of the most
influential contemporary works of (rather eclectic) art history,
Wilhelm Worringer's *Abstraction and Empathy*.[8] No one has yet been
able to prove that Lawrence did in fact read this book, which was
soon adopted by artists and art historians in Germany as a classic
statement, virtually a manifesto, of Expressionism. Running
athwart the Nietzsche line well known to Lawrence, the author
counterpoints two opposed world views: on the one hand the
humanist, post-Renaissance projection of an anthropocentric de-
sign upon the world, historically central to the tradition of European art; and on the other the alienating 'primitive' forms of

abstraction and geometric regularity which were, and are, cont-
rived with this degree of rigidity in order to control the incoherent
'organic' forces of the cosmos. Whether Lawrence had read Worringer or not, it is striking that his novel is built up on comparable
dualities in terms of what he calls 'life' and 'dissolution'; these terms
mean, roughly, a creative empathy with the world on the one hand,
and on the other the negative death drive which can also be a mode
of creation, as Romantic art shows us *passim*, but which in our more
neurotic age also unleashes unprecedented forces of destruction.

Already in relation to the sisters, then, and before the complex
saga of their men begins, the reader is made aware of a pattern of
complementarities as well as of opposites. Death is the condition of
life, as male is of female, negation of affirmation, and so on. Like
Blake, Baudelaire, or Dostoevsky, who constitute a major part of
Lawrence's 'tradition', he held firmly to a dialectical vision of life, to
the thesis that 'without contraries is no progression'. 'Innocence
and Experience' are the two 'contrary states of the human soul':
each contains, demands, and articulates the other; likewise Lawrence's 'river of Life' and 'river of Dissolution'.[9] And after all, if
Western civilisation, or a significant part of it, had not met its
Waterloo at the Somme, would it not have continued to live the life
of the opulent somnambulist evoked in the 'closed car at four'
section of the *Game of Chess*? Would the pub conversation among
the 'pawns' in society's heartless war games (whether at the front or
in the bedroom) ever have got written? And what of the extensive
borrowings from other cultures to plug the semiotic gaps in one's
own? It is precisely because the 'heritage' comes to us 'scrambled'
and piecemeal, in 'The Waste Land', in the form of quotations,
allusions, or parodies, that we can begin to make some sort of sense
of it and fit the fragments together into some provisional image of
our own 'experience'. 'Fear death by water?'[10] If the Father's 'death
by water' (which is a breaking down in order to reconstitute) had
never been symbolically enacted Ariel would have had no occasion
to sing his lovely song.

The Crich wedding that Ursula and Gudrun attend is one of
those 'nodal' points or vortices that set contradictory forces (feelings, ideas, relationships) in violent motion, and to that extent
forward whatever sort of 'plot' there is. We may or may not be
reminded of the delightful and rather fuddled wedding of Tom
and Lydia in *The Rainbow*, but at *this* wedding the slight irregularity

of the groom's late arrival only serves to underline the inordinately
self-conscious *forms* observed by people of good social class; we note
also how this carefully groomed good form exacerbates the bottled-
up feelings of rage, wounded pride, jealousy, and perverse desire
that beset the guests, or at any rate those we are asked to take an
interest in. Attention is drawn (as in the 'Breadalby' chapter) to the
'framing' of a certain kind of illusion, and to the roles and postures
adopted by the actors in this hieratic drama. Even the horses are in
on the game:

> But here was the bride's carriage, adorned with ribbons and
> cockades. Gaily the grey horses curvetted to their destination at
> the church-gate, a laughter in the whole movement. Here was
> the quick of all laughter and pleasure. The door of the carriage
> was thrown open, to let out the very blossom of the day. The
> people on the roadway murmured faintly with the discontented
> murmuring of a crowd. The father stepped out first into the air
> of the morning, like a shadow. He was a tall, thin, careworn man,
> with a thin black beard that was touched with grey. He waited at
> the door of the carriage patiently, self-obliterated. In the open-
> ing of the doorway was a shower of fine foliage and flowers, a
> whiteness of satin and lace, and a sound of a gay voice saying:
> "How do I get out?"[11]

In the passage, the impressionistic merging of individuals into
patterns of light and colour, and the discrete, forlorn gestures of
the father, point delicately but unanswerably towards the fact that
whereas the wedding games in *The Rainbow* helped people to be
themselves, by offering an unassertive social confirmation of their
identities, something different and 'decentred' is going on here. It
is much harder, in the world of this novel, to come to a perception
of who one is. The social roles of the participants in the scenario
are over-determined, and Lawrence, with the educated eye of the
working-class grammar school boy, discreetly but unerringly re-
cords this fact about the ruling classes, who are beginning to feel on
the defensive. The 'festivities' have about them an undertone of
suppressed violence, and it is suggested that this violence is
intrinsic to the ruling elite. Not for nothing is Gerald's totem the
'sinister' wolf, in Gudrun's view of him: we need little reminding
that he is the stuff of which the officer caste was made, the type of

those who sent thousands of young men to futile deaths. Hermione is self-consciously the 'alternative', the *Kulturträger*; not only is she the social equal of everyone present (and more equal than some), she also revels in her charisma as patroness of the arts in a dying culture. She, too, in her own way, is 'shoring up the fragments', in Eliot's phrase, collecting and assembling the 'bits'. Her real-life prototype, Lady Ottoline Morrell, surrounded herself, in fact, with some rather impressive cultural rejectamenta, as well as with some of the intellectuals who really counted in her time, in so far as there ever has been an English intelligentsia that counted (one of the problems the novel addresses itself to). What we observe at the wedding is unmistakably a power game, and may be another version of the 'condition of England' thesis whereby the 'grammar school hero' scores a moral Pyrrhic victory. Birkin, in other words, refuses to become another collectable (at least, that is *his* view of the situation). A rich and perverse fantasy life (*can* this be called 'experience'?) therefore surrounds the 'innocent' young couple, who have in some strange way defied the fates by their attractive spontaneity (cf. Birkin's discussion of what this consists in) in contracting a formal liaison without, it seems, first undergoing the obscure and devious rites of passage that Birkin, Ursula, Gerald, and Gudrun embark on. It is all quite different from *The Rainbow*, and much harsher. The hypertrophied social forms are simply irrelevant to the business of living; but what else is there? The question, as we have said, hangs heavy over the novel and its protagonists, whom we continually perceive as *performers* improvising the drama of their lives with a minimal script; and it seems as if there is no escaping this role playing, no 'private' space, though Birkin has the habit of fading out of the narrative occasionally, as if for a well-earned rest.

In this 'intermittent' life he is to some extent like Lawrence, whose 'flu' (tuberculosis) recurred at strategic, or not so strategic, intervals. Of course, when he is *not* there, he is much missed. At the beginning of Chapter Nineteen there is a characteristic observation about the devastating effects of his absence:

After his illness Birkin went to the south of France for a time. He did not write, nobody heard anything of him. Ursula, left alone, felt as if everything were lapsing out. There seemed to be no hope in the world. One was a tiny little rock with the tide of nothingness rising higher and higher. She herself was real, and only herself – just like a rock in a wash of flood-water. The rest was all nothingness. She was hard and indifferent, isolated in herself.[12]

This defines well the symbiotic nature of relationships in this novel. The conversation at the reception at Shortlands, the Criches' home, circles irritably and uneasily around questions of racial supremacy, productivity, power and violence:

"But," Gerald insisted, "you don't allow one man to take away his neighbour's living, so why should you allow one nation to take away the living from another nation?"

There was a long slow murmur from Hermione before she broke into speech, saying with a laconic indifference:

"It is not always a question of possessions, is it? It is not all a question of goods?"

Gerald was nettled by this implication of vulgar materialism.

"Yes, more or less," he retorted. "If I go and take a man's hat from off his head, that hat becomes a symbol of that man's liberty. When he fights me for his hat, he is fighting me for his liberty."

Hermione was nonplussed.

"Yes," she said, irritated.[13]

The assumption that there is nothing else to build life upon except violence and hatred, policed by the heavy arm of the law, prompts Birkin's deviant, if comic, behaviour as he drinks his champagne 'accidentally on purpose':

Birkin, thinking about race or national death, watched his glass being filled with champagne. The bubbles broke at the rim, the man withdrew, and feeling a sudden thirst at the sight of the fresh wine, Birkin drank up his glass. A queer little tension in the room roused him. He felt a sharp constraint.[14]

No wonder, then, that in the existential space between Gerald and Birkin (Cain and Abel, the builder of cities and the shepherd, or the industrialist and the school-inspector)[15] a tense sort of dialogue begins to take shape. It would be an understatement to say that Lawrence's novel is a contribution to the 'condition of England' question; *Howard's End*,[16] distinguished as it is, seems very low-key by comparison. But as this conversation makes apparent, the 'condition of England' at this particular point in time cannot be separated from the struggle for supremacy in Europe. It is therefore all the more ironic that it should be at Breadalby, Hermione's house (home of 'culture') that the conversation rattles like artillery fire; but at Shortlands, too, aggression keeps breaking through, showing us only too clearly where the war is really being lost and won, and even how it came about in the first place. It is also very clear why it matters so much to Birkin to affirm knowledge as power (as in 'Class-Room'), even when this is perceived as threatening by others. He belongs, after all, to that peculiarly disinherited class of 'aliens' (Matthew Arnold's term)[17] in English society – what passes among us for an intelligentsia. Somehow the 'intelligentsia of Great Britain' (title of the blistering attack by D. M. Mirsky)[18] seem to make a particularly poor showing, both inside and outside of Lawrence's novel, being (in *Women in Love*, and maybe not only in this novel) corrupt and venal. Yet one cannot manage without what Pound called the 'damned and despised literati'; they are, as Birkin indulgently says by way of initiating Gerald, 'negatively something'. These issues are most fully aired in the group of chapters ('Crème de Menthe', 'Totem', and 'Breadalby') which are set in the milieux of the Halliday entourage.

Lawrence, as we have seen, felt at home in the world of the visual arts. In *Women in Love*, as Keith Adritt has noted, painting and sculpture are invoked in order to illuminate character (the process is rather like James's use of internal 'reflectors', and to some extent the motivation is the same: with the disappearance of the omniscient narrator, it becomes very much harder to construct centres of consciousness, but the opportunities for diversifying points of view are correspondingly greater). According to Aldritt, Gudrun's liking for the small, the grotesque, and the diagrammatic is part of her 'camouflage', and is linked to an 'abstract' view of art comparable to Loerke's. Aldritt suggests that we are meant to contrast this with Birkin drawing the Chinese goose in order to discover 'what centres they live from'. There is a note of malice in Birkin's voice as he expounds his view of the goose, a malice clearly aimed at Hermione:

"I know what centres they live from – what they perceive and feel
– the hot, stinging centrality of a goose in the flux of cold water
and mud – the curious bitter stinging heat of a goose's blood,
entering their own blood like an inoculation of corruptive fire –
fire of the cold-burning mud – the lotus mystery."[19]

We are also, Aldritt claims, meant to contrast Gudrun and Loerke's
self-conscious art-critical dialogues with Birkin's gut response to
Picasso and his 'almost wizard, sensuous apprehension of the
earth'. Some of the works of art mentioned do more, we know,
than just illuminate character: such, for instance, are the West
African statues and the two works by Loerke, each constituting a
'major crisis in the story' (thus Aldritt, who also notes that 'primitive' statues form part of the 'initial enterprise and the tradition of
Cubism'). Aldritt's arguments are sound as far as they go, but they
are also misleading in so far as they try to pin Lawrence down to a
single thesis or 'line', i.e. that modern art has taken a wrong turning
after Cézanne by rejecting a 'human' perspective. *Women in Love*, as
a novel, is a collage of small, diagrammatic, and often grotesque
episodes. Whatever else it may be, the goose is a 'fleur du mal', a
creature of the mud, as nowadays we all are, more or less,
according to Birkin. But the goose represents an intensity of
experience in dissolution. Copying a drawing of it (it was a present
from the Chinese ambassador, so Birkin's appropriation of it is a
sort of subversive response to Hermione's 'collectables') is a way of
coming to terms with creation in dissolution. Of course it is true
that Lawrence *did* take issue, vociferously, with Roger Fry and the
proponents of 'Significant Form', and fought to rescue his beloved
Cézanne from the abstractionists; but given the vacuity of Fry's
theories (despite his alert critical sense and the charm of his style)
this is not at all surprising. Lawrence's fascination with the complex
impersonality, the pronounced anti-humanism, of the work of the
Italian Futurists, should warn us against bracketing him too easily
with an aesthetics of empathy. Loerke is an interesting case; even if
we can agree that he is a self-seeking opportunist, his intervention
in Gudrun and Gerald's relationship is largely catalytic in that it
was almost inevitable that Gudrun would leave Gerald in any case;
and as to Loerke's arguments on art (his sculpture, he says, is a
'picture of nothing'; Ursula confuses the 'relative world of action
with the absolute world of art'; art should serve industry as it once

served the Church) they at least make a better showing than
Ursula's anecdotal commentaries. In the end, of course, he *is*
wrong, because pictures of nothing turn into pictures of something
in the process of being received and decoded.

Which is what happens in the three chapters given over to the
world of art in the novel, where Lawrence creates a kind of
conceptual space, by analogy with Cézanne and the Futurists,
around the icon of the woman in labour, the embodiment of
incompleteness. Lawrence's comments on Cézanne are extensive
and combative, and sometimes they sound like an Expressionist
manifesto; but their essence is contained in the following propositions:

> The eye sees only fronts, and the mind, on the whole, is satisfied
> with fronts. But intuition needs all-aroundness, and instinct
> needs insideness. The true imagination is for ever curving round
> to the other side, to the back of presented appearance.[20]

Cézanne

> sets the unmoving material world into motion. Walls twitch and
> slide, chairs bend or rear up a little, cloths curl like burning
> paper.[21]

The placing of the 'primitive' carving in a resonant space is an
instance of the 'Chladni's Plate' method of composition, and a way
of 'curving round to the other side', responding to the silent music.
Compositionally, it strongly suggests Cézanne's *Still Life with Plaster
Cupid*, one of his most dynamic paintings, which is itself similar in
important formal respects to Boccioni's bottle (which it also superficially resembles). If one were to try to identify the 'sand grains' in
this particular sequence of Lawrence's novel, they might be located
in the 'loose' social affiliations of artistic Bohemia, which is amorphous enough to contain the off-duty captain of industry and
school inspector as well as the artist's model (there is a snide
comment at Shortlands to the effect that society has now become
more egalitarian). But they might equally be the scatter of fashionable exoticism, and eroticism, the kinds of 'freedom' (how real?)
offered by a rootless lifestyle, the self-conscious nudity and talk of
primitivism, and Birkin's bile ('Crème de Menthe', the typically

laconic chapter title, is picked up in 'Birkin was drinking something green'). Cèzanne's canvas similarly presents a range of discrete motifs, contained within their own 'microspaces',[22] but his plaster cupid, swivelling vertiginously, nakedly emergent on its table like Boccioni's bottle, generates a kind of centripetal force that holds all the different picture planes together in an ambiguous tension of real and represented worlds (including the *other* picture that has the back of its stretcher to the viewer).[23]

A strictly comparable impersonal dynamic is generated in *Women in Love* by the sculpture of the woman in labour, which is a particularly decisive compositional intervention, or stroke of the bow against the metal plate. An icon, as we have seen, of the whole novel (bearing down, waiting) she generates a Futurist 'field of force' that draws in a wide range of significant elements. The dominant motif is primitivism itself: evidently extremes have met (as Worringer discovered) when African and Oceanic carvings became the inspiration of Expressionism, Cubism, Futurism and other manifestations of a highly evolved painterly tradition. Gerald (who impresses Minette with his explorer's tales of the 'savages' in his Amazon trip) gets locked in a tense debate with Birkin over whether this is art, unable or unwilling as he is to 'experience' (the current jargon 'relate to' is rather apt) the intense knowledge in dissolution that it represents, and which has a lot to do with him. Halliday has a taste for these things, but cannot begin to understand their resonances. The figure in the sand grains mutates imperceptibly to encompass Minette. Gerald recognises her in this sculpted icon of arrest, but cannot look deeper and see himself imaged there too. Minette, the 'violated slave' of Halliday and Gerald, seems to enjoy, in some perverse way, her humiliation and rejection. She is a disturbing presence for Gerald, who (characteristically) would like to pay her for spending the night with him, as if to 'finalise' the relationship.

In such ways do the real and represented worlds interact dialogically. The resonances from their interaction reach deeper and deeper into the fictional world – as far, at least, as the desperate 'Moony' chapter, stirring a 'primitive' fear in Birkin as he hovers on the brink of proposing to Ursula, but has to fight against profound resistances and emanations of the 'magna mater':

Thousands of years ago, that which was imminent in himself

must have taken place in these Africans: the goodness, the holiness, the desire for creation and productive happiness must have lapsed, leaving the single impulse for knowledge in one sort, mindless progressive knowledge through the senses, knowledge arrested and ending in the senses, mystic knowledge in disintegration and dissolution, knowledge such as the beetles have which live purely within the world of corruption and cold dissolution.[24]

The most crucial episodes in the novel make use of this kind of 'diagrammatic' scenario to deliver a powerful expressive charge. Birkin is by no means a privileged onlooker at these 'dumb shows'; even when he seems to be actually scripting the scenario, as in *Mino*, a play of reader perspectives within perspectives (fighting cats are to Birkin and Ursula as Birkin and Ursula are to Birkin's landlady) undercuts his rhetoric. This is one of the passages cited by Kate Millett as evidence of Lawrence's aggressive sexism, and the quarrelsomeness of the two lovers is, of course, characteristic, and may be felt by some to be excessive. But it is only by quoting it out of context that Millett manages to present it as evidence of Lawrence's contempt for women (rather in the way that, in the bad old days, Shakespeare-fanciers would cite a particular speech or soliloquy out of context as evidence of Shakespeare's 'philosophy of life'). This practice, akin to fundamentalist readings of the Bible, ignores questions of tone, attitude, dialogism, the distribution of meanings. When it comes down to it, it is not even too hot on content (or 'ideology'), despite the fact that this is overtly its concern. Of course Birkin's tone is immoderate; but here as elsewhere he is conspicuously less the prisoner and the agent of the death drive than Gerald, who, in the sequence that Russell filmed so well, goes from the cemetery straight to Gudrun's bed and, like a frozen plant suddenly thawing and bursting, injects his venemous sap into her (cf. the climax of Baudelaire's poem *A celle qui est trop gaie*). By doing so he finds a fragile sense of relief and renewal, while she is left trying to ease herself free of his inert bulk. This kind of fraught conjunction will repeat itself many times. But equally, the point is often made that Birkin, who is also a 'fleur du mal', is not immune to the sickness of the age: it is simply his special gift to see it, intermittently, for what it is. 'Moony', the crucial chapter already referred to, is a good instance of this, and another interesting specimen of, or on, the sanded tray.

Lawrence's battle with 'the mother in the mind' never quite ended. In this Gothic, quasi-operatic set piece, he places the ailing Birkin, his attenuated double, face to face with the glittering surface of Willey Water, which has already claimed its victims. Picking up on the image of 'withering in the bud', from the first chapter of the novel, Birkin, in a demented parody of the fertility rites of Frazer's *Golden Bough* (cf. 'The Waste Land') casts dead flower-husks into the water and intones what is probably the principal *Leitmotiv* of the novel, and one horribly close to Lawrence's heart, and his own situation, during the war years: 'You can't go away. . . There *is* no away.' His mental agitation issues in a curse against the creative/destructive Syria Dea (whose votaries, among other things, ritually castrated themselves); and he throws stones at the reflection of Cybele's planet, the moon (evoked as a cuttle-fish or polyp, like the lanterns of 'Water-party', connoting death). There is a violent transformation of the enigmatic two-dimensional surface of Chladni's Plate. As the stones strike the water, they shatter the image of the moon, which splits and reforms, writhing 'in blind effort'. Some motifs here, and the destructive/regenerative thrust, recall 'What the Thunder Said', the last part of Eliot's 'The Waste Land'. Eliot said (though without any suggestion it might be a problem, still less *his* problem) that all the women of his great poem were 'one woman'. Cybele is for Birkin a kind of split image of both Hermione and Ursula; but beyond mere 'personality' the moon goddess codes both the destructive and the creative parts of the 'anima', or female emanation from the male self, and this is the site of Birkin's battle. The image of a kaleidoscope is invoked: the split moon is also the split psyche and the fissured surface of Lawrence's novel, like a kind of shattered mirror that still just holds together. The fragments insist on reconstituting themselves in a new order, alternately 'rose-like' (a soothing *Gestalt*) and unsettling like a polyp (again an echo of the violent imagery of 'Water-Party'). As in 'The Waste Land', the traumatic rupture of a culture, of a 'mind' (whether Eliot's own or the notional 'mind of Europe' he constructs) releases unpredictable energies. The 'death by water' imagery of 'The Waste Land' contains a set of themes that are closely analogous to those of Lawrence's novel.

Briefly, there is a rapprochement between Birkin and Ursula, and a startling flashback to the African carving with its resonating succession of images (the 'death-break' Gerald, snow), but Birkin's efforts at doing the right thing, asking the burnt-out Will for his daughter's hand in marriage, are pointless and premature. He is still afraid of giving himself in love; in a way, still afraid of the woman's power; hence 'Gladiatorial', which follows according to the inner dynamic of the sanded tray, and yokes together the 'condition of England' theme with an exploration of the wilder shores of love (a discarded preface reminds us that the novel as originally conceived was to have had a more explicit homosexual element). At the time of the novel's publication this episode terrified some reviewers (or perhaps they pretended that it did). Since Russell's vigorous screen version, it has probably lost its power to shock. But like Ursula's venture in lesbian love in *The Rainbow*, it dramatises a movement of recoil, and has little follow-through. There is no way of transcending the novelistic world of 'interrupted gestures', which is also, Lawrence suggests, the modern world (cf. Benjamin's essay on Brecht's alienation effect, which, with an ostensibly 'progressive' purpose, shows us what it means to be all process and no product). There is, quite simply, 'no away', though Birkin does, as we have seen, occasionally 'drop out' in the time-honoured Romantic fashion from a novel which must have been exhausting to play the lead in. Lawrence continued to pursue his vanishing cultural-Utopian mirage (which led him deeper into the contradictions of his own experience, and ours, rather than to any viable version of a promised land). But the note of irresolution on which *Women in Love* ends, or fails to end, prepares the way for a different venture, and one which we have only recently acquired the means to evaluate properly as the significant new departure it is in Lawrence's *œuvre*.

5

Carnivalising the Midlands

The Lost Girl and *Mr Noon*

The two novels that 'really' follow *Women in Love* have a chequered history, and this is why they have not been known and enjoyed as they deserve to be. When *The Lost Girl* was published in 1920, five years had elapsed since the suppression of *The Rainbow*, and much blood had flowed under the bridge. The new novel was well received. The *Manchester Guardian* reviewer, Edward Garnett (recipient of the intricate commentary on 'old stable egos'), was pleasantly surprised to find it 'firm in drawing, light and witty in texture, charmingly fresh in style and atmosphere', and commended its 'democratic irreverence'. *The Nation* liked the 'absence of feverishness' and of 'sexual preoccupation'. *The Westminster Gazette* was struck by the way

> Mr Lawrence's muse has mated with Mr Arnold Bennett or with Mr Compton Mackenzie, or with both.

Virginia Woolf's review concentrated on the realistic rendering of provincial life, as if nothing else much was going on, and Bennett himself expressed admiration for the novel in a letter to his (and Lawrence's) agent: it would 'be great if it had a real theme and some construction. This man is a genius, and is far and away the best of the younger school.'[1] For a long time, this 'anomalous' work was accounted for genetically. Leavis, who pointed out the affinity with *Hard Times*, attributed the lack of any 'compelling total significance' of the fact that 'the book was written during widely separate phases of Lawrence's life'. On this view there are three stages: the Woodhouse material, described by Leavis as 'a remarkable rendering of English provincial life' of the Bennett sort,

76

'though, being the work of a great creative genius, it is utterly beyond Bennett's achievement'; the parts reminiscent of the 'nightmare' material of *Kangaroo*, where Ciccio becomes an undesirable alien and private detectives hound the troupe of actors as they hounded Lawrence and Frieda; and the Italian material, cast in the mould of travelogue and written from immediate experience of Italy but set earlier in time.[2]

Leavis, of course, did not have all the facts. The first draft of the novel has disappeared, and the short remaining fragment of another reworking is largely immaterial. John Worthen concludes after a much better informed survey of the evidence that the *whole* of the text published in 1920 is new work, completely rewritten: and this is consistent with Lawrence's practice in other novels.[3] But this only makes the stylistic anomalies of *The Lost Girl* more puzzling, after the full-blown Modernism of *Women in Love*. Why go back to Dickens, or to the realism of *Sons and Lovers*, which Lawrence had rejected in 1913 as 'full of sensation and presentation'?[4] Why should Lawrence be writing like Bennett at all? A letter of some years earlier may help us to give an answer to these questions:

> I have read *Anna of the Five Towns* today, because it is stormy weather. For five months I have scarcely seen a word of English print, and to read it makes me feel fearfully queer. I don't know where I am ... today, to be in Hanley, and to read almost my own dialect, makes me feel quite ill. I hate England and its hopelessness. I hate Bennett's resignation. Tragedy ought to be a great kick at misery. But *Anna of the Five Towns* seems like an acceptance – so does all the modern stuff since Flaubert. I hate it. I want to wash again quick, wash off England, the oldness and grubbiness and despair.[5]

The initial motivation for writing *The Lost Girl* is thus not to imitate Bennett, whom Lawrence had a low opinion of, but to compose a riposte, and cock a snook at England. The keynote of this letter is contradiction: England/Italy, English/Italian, 'resignation'/ Nietzschean tragic vitalism. The patchwork effects in *The Lost Girl* derive, I think, from the considerable cultural defamiliarisation Lawrence was experiencing at the time. As a novel it is peculiarly preoccupied with asking questions about 'voicing': who speaks, and from what standpoint; what kinds of writing are available in this historical and geographical location and moment.

Bennett was, for Lawrence, (as his letters show us), the commercially successful writer *par excellence* (Bennett sent Lawrence an anonymous gift of £40 in November 1915, and in 1917 there was talk of him raising a private subscription to support the publication of *Women in Love*). Indifferent as Lawrence was to money matters, he was beginning to feel some resentment at the success of lesser writers, and to feel that he, too, could write a best seller (though in one letter he expressed his fear that his new novel may be 'too commercial' for Secker's refined tastes). Additionally, Lawrence's satirical muse (cf. *Women in Love* and *St Mawr*) was still unsatisfied. It does not do the novel justice to talk, as John Worthen does, of the frivolity of the first part and lack of commitment of the second; and when he says, disapprovingly, that the heroine is 'a centre used by the narrator rather than a created life' he is misreading (threadbare terms like 'created life' continue to bedevil Lawrence criticism). It is the narrator who particularly troubles Worthen; some characters, he says, have no existence outside of his 'dominant, flippant rhetoric'. But it was precisely some such reincorporation and foregrounding of the tone of the speaking voice that was vitally necessary if Lawrence was to engage with the 'objectivity' of Bennett's naturalism, and respond to the 'talking and singing' voices of the Italian streets while he read dutifully on, in the rain, through the 'resignation' of Bennett's text.

Henry James characterised Bennett with great skill in *The New Novel*.[6] Bracketing him with Wells, James speaks of his 'extraordinary mass of gathered and assimilated knowledge'. Bennett writes 'because he knows', and the 'new' is, for him, simply 'an appetite for closer notation'. The lack of 'inner life' that Worthen finds in *The Lost Girl* is a *sine qua non* of Bennett's naturalism:

> . . . a general scene and a cluster of agents deficient to a peculiar degree in properties that might interfere with a desirable density of illustration – deficient, that is, in such connections as might carry the imagination off to come sport on its own account.

The phrase 'sport on its own account' is, as we shall see, highly apposite to Lawrence's novel. With Bennett, says James, we find 'perfect harmony' between 'subject and author', but perfection of this sort is bound to provoke anxieties:

These are the circumstances of the interest – we see, we see; but where is the interest itself, where and what is its centre, and how are we to measure it in relation to *that*?

Readerly pleasure disappears in the absence of an 'effect of expression'. James's account of *The Old Wives' Tale* is so germane that I will transcribe it at length

> The canvas is covered, ever so closely and vividly covered, by the exhibition of innumerable small facts and aspects, at which we assist with the most comfortable sense of their substantial truth. The sisters, and more particularly the less adventurous, are at home in their author's mind, they sit and move at their ease in the square chamber of his attention, to a degree beyond which the production of that ideal harmony between creature and creator could scarcely go, and all by an art of demonstration so familiar and so 'quiet' that the truth and the poetry, to use Goethe's distinction, melt utterly together and we see no difference between the subject of the show and the showman's manner, about it. This felt identity of the elements . . . becomes . . . a source for us of abject confidence, confidence *truly* so abject in the solidity of every appearance that it may be said to represent our whole relation to the work and completely to exhaust our reaction upon it.[7]

'Square' is right: in *Anna* the Sunday-school yard, in *The Old Wives' Tale* St Luke's Square, are models of the mind, and houses are much-discussed determinants of identity (which is largely a matter of what people think of you, 'status', in other words). Point of view is fixed, 'objective', and purely social. Bennett's pseudo-objectivity is just one manifestation of those many 'deletions' that David Lodge finds typical of his metonymic prose. Patriarchal authority is masked as received truth, yet one cannot help observing that, if a woman's lot is (on the whole) renunciation, this could have something to do with man's lot being, as the novels seem to tell us, to get rich and buy lots of things. James noted, for instance, the rapt accumulation of narrative detail which mediates this fascination with the accumulation of money and property. Beyond a residual 'nonconformist' anxiety, there is actually no point of reference beyond the world of cash values. This goes with a marked materialising (or naturalising) of states of mind, a concretising of subjectivity à la Flaubert. Alan Sillitoe, in his introduction to a recent edition of *The Old Wives' Tale*, cites Sophia's first feelings of love: 'She was drunk; thoughts were tumbling about in her brain like cargo loose in a rolling ship.' Flaubertian, too, is the long description of Tellwright's dresser; it is an index of hard work (that of Anna and her mother), of order (the paralysis that Tellwright's miserly dictatorship has induced in Anna's soul) and of the approval of the next man to lay claim to Anna (Mynors reflects that 'there is nothing to beat a clean, straight kitchen, and there never will be'). But the narrator's irony, while maintaining a critical distance, endorses an acceptance of the status quo and the values that sustain it. See, for instance, Bennett's evocation of Anna's reaction to her discovery of her fortune:

> Practically, Anna could not believe that she was rich; and in fact she was not rich – she was merely a fixed point through which moneys that she was unable to arrest passed with the rapacity of trains.

Striking as this image is, there is no awareness on the narrator's part that it could undermine the stability of cash values, or bear witness to the real nature of the sexual politics of his world (it is an image of rape).[8]

All this should be kept in mind when we compare Lawrence's Woodhouse to Bennett's pottery towns. There are analogies on the level of character, action and description, even one or two close verbal echoes (the 'Slaves of the Underworld' passage, as we shall see, seems to derive from Bennett's description of the Price house in *Anna of the Five Towns*, though it is also a stylised echo of the 'expressionist' world of *Women in Love*). Both novels deal with the rise and fall of a small business. In each novel, a protagonist is sent abroad to provide a new perspective on England. But Lawrence's novel is what Harold Bloom might call a 'strong reading' of Bennett, i.e. one that takes issue with the actual *mode of production* of its forerunner, the thing that, in the original, is so carefully effaced. James's phrase about 'the showman's manner' is highly germane. To put it more theoretically (via Todorov),[9] Lawrence is setting 'énonciation' against 'énoncé' (the 'two equal linguistic realities, that of the characters and that of the narrator–listener duality') rather than concealing the difference under the guise of 'perfect harmony between subject and author' (James). At every stage, Lawrence's text draws attention to its own coming into being, its 'mode of production', by means of a gesturing, self-dramatising narrator who, like a music-hall entertainer, enacts the disconcerting switches of code that frustrate and disorientate passive readerly expectations. In other words, the discontinuities that critics have noted in *The Lost Girl* have been put there in order to dramatise the 'crisis of the subject' with which the novel engages thematically.

The main 'metafictional mirror' in the novel is what Eikhenbaum calls (in relation to Gogol) the 'skaz illusion'.[10] Dominating the Woodhouse scenes, and combining with the play-acting of the theatre folk (as if the narrator were a travelling showman trying out new parts – including, in the case of Mr May and James, some that look transvestite) the *skaz* illusion may be located in an unmotivated interplay of written and spoken modes, the phenomenon which Eikhenbaum calls 'sonic gesturing'. In the unstable realism of the Russian nineteenth century, 'skaz' indicates the active presence of dialect and folktale as well as incongruous 'high' cultural interlinguas and the tenuous survival of baroque rhetorical and compositional modes (illusionism). 'Sonic gesturing' is at once evident in the punctuation of *The Lost Girl*. The Cambridge editor notes that

> Lawrence often followed a full stop, question mark or exclamation mark before beginning the next sentence with a capital letter, e.g. 'job. – But' (2.9). His typist occasionally and the typesetter consistently omitted the dash, which has been restored in this edition.

The paragraph referred to reads in full:

> However it be, it is a tragedy. Or perhaps it is not. Perhaps these unmarried women of the middle-class are the famous sexless Workers of our ant-industrial society, of which we hear so much. Perhaps all they lack is an occupation: in short, a job. – But perhaps we might hear their own opinion, before we lay the law down.[11]

This device is closely related to the use of digression and of improvisation, as well as to the ideology of the novel in terms of its

treatment of the question of women's rights. In the theatrical
episodes, the name 'Natcha-Kee-Tawara' is itself a sonic gesture,
perhaps echoing Chateaubriand's *Les Natchez*. As with other incan-
tational uses of language in Lawrence's work, the name connotes
the charades Lawrence still played as an adult, and a kind of
polymorphous 'jouissance' (cf. the playing at Indians in *The Plumed
Serpent*). The device is motivated by Alvina's incorporation into a
(slightly louche) world of childlike irresponsibility (the analogy with
the horse-riding in *Hard Times* has often been noticed) which her
upbringing has denied her (her father had a monopoly of it). 'Sonic
gesture' relates directly to the use of foreign languages in the text.
When Alvina is received into the pseudo-tribal order of the
Natchas (a parody of a matriarchal family and a carnivalesque
'alternative' to bourgeois patriachy) the event is marked by a comic
incantation, a Bohemian or 'Apache' parody of family 'together-
ness':

> "We are one tribe, one nation – say it."
> "We are one tribe, one nation", repeated Alvina.
> "Say all," cried Madame.
> "We are one tribe, one nation –" they shouted, with varying
> accent.
> "Good!" said Madame. "And no nation do we know but the
> nation of the Hirondelles."
> "No nation do we know but the nation of the Hirondelles",
> came the ragged chant of the strong male voices, resonant and
> gay with mockery.[12]

There is also a ritual renaming in which Alvina becomes Allaye
(her double identity answering to the theatrical 'doubleness' of a
text where even the narrator is playing a part). This seems to be a
creative misunderstanding of Vaali, Madame's name for her,
apparently from Crèvecoeur. When the name becomes the property of the multilingual group it is transformed first into 'viale', then
into the French 'allée' by Ciccio (who here speaks French), with an
erotic overtone which could have been threatening in any other,
less supportive, context. Madame's colourful distortions of standard English correspond to the transgressiveness of the group in
other ways and link up with Lawrence's fascination with translation
as an almost 'androgynous' interpretation of roles and identities.[13]

The multinationality of the group is reiterated and reworked through heteroglossia and transcodings. The narrator, for instance, notes Ciccio's dependence on gesture:

> Gesture and grimace were instantaneous, and spoke worlds of things, if you would but accept them.

As in the 'Rabbit' chapter of *Women in Love*, altercations in mixed foreign languages link personal and political tensions, catching a distant resonance of the coming war. Multilingualism relates directly to theatrical performance in Madame's rapid switches, especially when she is ill:

> So Madame moaned in four languages as she posed pallid in her armchair. Usually she spoke in French only, with her young men. But this was an extra occasion.

Two more *skaz* elements reinforce the reader's awareness of the conditions of the text's production: the use of dialect and the use of hyperbole. Both constitute a 'dance of the speech organs' (Shklovsky) and an impedance of narrative. Dialect is not used extensively, but considerable significance attaches to the key chapter 'Two Women Die', where Alvina descends to the underworld:

> "Ay, that's the road it goes, Miss Huffen – Yis, Yo'll see th'roof theer bellies down a bit – s'loose. – No you dunna get th'puddin' stones i' this pit – s'not deep enough. Eh, they come down on you plumb, as if th'roof had laid its egg on you. – "

and so on. It is done, of course, for reasons very different from Bennett's departures from standard English.

Hyperbole takes many forms. The 'slaves of the underworld' section, which stands out like an intruder introduced from Gudrun's expostulations in *Women in Love*, in fact echoes Bennett: behind the Price house

> could be seen an expanse of grey-green field, with a few abandoned pit-shafts scattered over it. These shafts, imperfectly protected by ruinous masonry, presented an appearance strangely sinister and forlorn, raising visions in the mind of dark

and mysterious depths peopled with miserable ghosts of those
who had toiled there in the days when to be a miner was to be a
slave.

Lawrence:

> Slaves of the underworld! She watched the swing of the grey
> colliers along the pavement with a new fascination, hypnotised
> by a new vision. Slaves – the underground trolls and iron-
> workers, magic, mischievous, and enslaved, of the ancient stor-
> ies. But tall – the miners seemed to her to loom tall and grey, in
> their enslaved magic. . . .

It is that fascinating s/he that is half an 'I' that Roger Fowler
notices, making a dialogue of the descriptive writing, turning it into
a drama of consciousness (rather than an 'objective' fact) in a set of
changing subject positions. If this passage *is* an echo of Bennett, as
it seems to be, Lawrence's transformation of it is wholly characteristic. In Bennett's severely metonymic style narrative sequences are
held in place by significant 'things' (like the plate of *Anna of the Five
Towns*, or Mr Povey's tooth in *The Old Wives' Tale*). Lawrence's
narrator, on the other hand, deals like a fairground juggler with
material objects. The treatment of money, again, is a case in point:
for Bennett, cash relations determine all relations, and cash values
are absolute. Thus Sophia, escaping mercantile St Luke's Square, is
transported to an equally money-minded Paris, described with
almost no historical depth:

> Though Sophia continued to increase her prices, and was now
> selling her stores at an immense profit, she never approached the
> prices current outside. She was very indignant against the
> exploitation of Paris by its shopkeepers, who had vast supplies of
> provender, and were hoarding for the rise. But the force of their
> example was too great for her to ignore it entirely; she contented
> herself with about half their gains.[14]

Over *The Lost Girl*'s well-documented commercial *milieux*, on the
other hand, hangs an air of unreality. The succession of sales that
mark the decline and fall of Manchester House have a range of
complex functions (not least, they register subtle changes of taste

and of self-image in the little community): and although James is, on one level, just Lawrence's equivalent of Bennett's miserly Tellwright, on another level he is a mysterious individual pursuing his own obscure objects of desire. The narrator has to guess creatively at what he might be up to, through a dense constellation of shifting metaphors:

> James Houghton had become so stingy it was like an inflammation in him. A silver sixpence had a pale and celestial radiance which he could not forego, a nebulous whiteness which made him feel he had heaven in his hold. How then could he let it go. Even a brown penny seemed alive and pulsing with mysterious blood, potent, magical. He loved the flock of his busy pennies, in the shop, as if they had been divine bees bringing him sustenance from the infinite. But the pennies he saw dribbling away in household expenses troubled him acutely, as if they were live things leaving his fold.[15]

James's 'monetarism' is thus subtly linked (through imagery of transcendence and salvation) with the Protestant ethic, while at the same time adumbrating, through the manner of its narrating, a larger critique of the absorption of human values by cash values. There is also no mistaking the fact that James's love of money displaces a deeper need. The peculiar magic of money is developed at the end of the chapter called (with overtones of the chapel) 'Houghton's Last Endeavour'. After the first night of his new theatre he brushes Alvina aside and rushes off with the takings to count them in private:

> He swept his table clear, and then, in an expert fashion, he seized handfuls of coin and piled them in little columns on his board. There was an army of fat pennies, a dozen to a column, along the back, rows and rows of fat brown rank-and-file. In front of these, rows of slim halfpence, like an advance-guard. And commanding all, a stout column of half-crowns, a few stoutish and important florin-figures, like generals and colonels . . . He loved to see the pence, like innumerable pillars of cloud, standing waiting to lead on into the wilderness of unopened resource, while the silver, as pillars of light, should guide the way down the long night of fortune. Their weight sank sensually into his

muscle, and gave him gratification. The dark redness of bronze, like full-blooded fleas, seemed alive and pulsing, the silver was magic as if winged.[16]

James is a little boy playing soldiers, but his game is shadowed by impotence masquerading as megalomania, Biblical righteousness (the *Rainbow* imagery) in the guise of patriarchal power; and this on the eve of war. Lawrence's images of performing fleas and quicksilver, suggesting *Hard Times* and circus entertainment, where nothing is what it seems to be, gently mock James. A similar instance, with a marked *skaz* virtuosity, is the image whereby Albert Witham, one of Alvina's rejected suitors, becomes wholly effaced by the rhetorical figure through which he is evoked. Witham is judged to be 'a queer fish' or 'an odd fish' (the 'old maids' that Lawrence speaks up for are 'odd women', in Gissing's phrase). It was as if 'one was looking at him through the glass wall of an aquarium', he lives in a 'dumb, aqueous silence'. 'Strange it was, like Alice in Wonderland' says the narrator, and indeed we are reminded of the games Carroll plays with Darwin's evolutionary hypothesis. The metaphor displaces the object to which it ostensibly refers. As a dimension of popular entertainment, the extravagance of this conjuring trick forms part of Lawrence's riposte to Bennett's four-square naturalism.

It will not do, therefore, to say that *The Lost Girl* was written quickly to make money (Worthen). Along with *Mr Noon*, it represents a new venture into a very 'chancy' kind of writing. It may not transgress the same taboos as *The Rainbow* and *Women in Love*, but like *Mr Noon* it is a 'hair-raiser'.[17] Does James dress up in women's clothes? Village gossip would like to think so. Certainly Mr May plays Madame's role in the Red Indian charade, and we know that Maurice Magnus (his real-life prototype, who Lawrence admired) was homosexual. The hint of transvestism is just one of several elements of sexual chanciness in the book. Apart from the (mildly) obscene fun and games of Alvina's acceptance into the tribe (another change of identity) there is the sexual ambivalence of her dominant, rather 'male'(?) roles in relation to her dependant lovers (including, of course, Ciccio, though I cannot see that lasting). With gentle but telling satire the older women, Miss Frost and Miss Pinnegar, are shown as quietly running things behind the back of James, whose extravagance and irresponsibility constitute a perpetual threat to the family fortunes. James and Mr May, with their proprietorial ambitions (coal mine and cinema) are comically trying to affirm a virility no one needs: May likes to call the building an 'erection' ('merely temporary', he adds). The debate about the relative merits of cinema and music-hall in Chapter Eight, where Madame castigates film as appealing to 'impertinent curiosity' while in music-hall there is a 'feeling of the heart' generated by a community (cf. Eliot on Marie Lloyd),[18] may not be of any great merit in itself; but in the 'splitting' (or doubling) of the identity of subject/object in music-hall (there *is* no passive audience, everyone is a performer) is fascinating: transvestism, polyglotism, Alvina/ Allaye, the Midlands/Italy, Woodhouse/Woodlouse – to borrow Madame's Freudian parapraxis – the whole fictional world is 'polymorphous' and decentred ('no total significance', said Leavis). And more or less the same is true of *Mr Noon*.

Mr Noon probably started life as a rejected fragment of *The Lost Girl* in 1913, but like its companion piece it was completely rewritten later. The first part took eight weeks of 1920, the second was written, but never quite finished, in 1921. Lawrence saw Part Two as 'a bit startling'[19] and 'a bit of a hair-raiser'; the first part was published on its own after Lawrence's death, and the second part lost. Reviewers noted both 'gusto' and 'irony' in the treatment of Mr Noon's courtship rites in Woodhouse (i.e. the town bears the same name as in *The Lost Girl*) and one H. J. Davis[20] chose to introduce a comparison with Arnold Bennett, though like the reviewers of *The Lost Girl* he missed the point, which lies in the differences as much as the similarities:

> The scene and the talk is as exactly reproduced as in a Bennett novel, and produces an effect of realism.

As with *The Lost Girl*, the *skaz* illusion is carefully fostered, as material of a sometimes very personal and autobiographical kind is tossed up in the air, and kept in perpetual motion, by an intrepid juggler/narrator who never loses touch with the grain of the living voice. Dialogue predominates: there are pages of almost nothing else, and the 'Dear reader' or 'Gentle reader' is drawn into it (this reader is overtly constructed as feminine about half-way through, as one in the eye for 'the sterner sex', since men, we are told, want to hold on to their sentimental illusions about love like a baby clinging to a dummy). The pastiche Bennett material has been taken several steps further in the direction of a disturbingly exact, and rather pro-female, satire upon sexual mores. This in turn leads to a scarcely fictionalised account of Lawrence's early days with Frieda that lets a lot of randy cats out of the bag. These passages are particularly startling in that so little fuss attaches to Gilbert's discovery of Joanna's unashamed, and somewhat indiscriminately exercised, sexuality. Nothing could be more different from the morally strenuous autobiographical writing of *Sons and Lovers*, despite the marginal overlap in subject matter. Moreover, although Noon himself is perfunctorily represented as a composer (among other things), 'Art' scarcely brushes the surface of this text. 'Lucky' Noon (a man at his zenith) is glossed as German 'Nun', 'now', on account of his determination to seize the moment[21] (but perhaps an inverse echo of English 'nun' as well, since he is made to look like one, beside the sexually adventurous Joanna). He is also 'No-one', the English nobody who walked off with the wife of a distinguished American doctor/English professor who was also the daughter of a Baron; perhaps also 'not-one', since 'he loved the world in its multiplicity',[22] Lawrence therefore, as the 'trespasser' in both parts of the novel, the rank outsider, has good reason to play his carnivalesque[23] games with hierarchies, codes, mental and bodily functions, and reader–writer relations.

Like the narrator of *The Lost Girl*, this narrator juggles ad lib with images and phrases that spark off witty or bizarre trains of thought, dramatising *énonciation* and directing our attention as much to process as to product. The most sustained is the set of variations on the theme of the 'spoon', an acceptable mode of transgression (i.e. of the 'official' sexual morality) that nevertheless saddens by virtue of the inevitability with which it leads from brief hole-and-corner encounters, which bring little satisfaction, to years of stable married life, like the Goddards', that may offer content-ment but give little hope of change or adventure. The narrator rings some changes on the 'spooning' theme, shifting it away from the iconography of popular song (Noon/spoon/moon/June) to-wards, on the one hand, what kinds of deprivation it signifies for the society that practises it (especially for women), and on the other towards the laughable or painful emotional tangles that result from a practice that is half institutionalised (courtship) and half-condemned (licence). The first part of the novel ends with a chapter called 'The Interloper' where a lively comic irony plays over the incongruities and absurdities that result when double, or treble, standards are applied. There is, for instance, the fine climax of the scene that brings Emmie (pregnant by Noon?), Noon himself, and the Romantic suitor Walter George together, with a sort of 'there but for the grace of God' relish on Lawrence's part:

> From below they heard the clink of tea-spoons and smelled the steam of stirring cocoa. And suddenly Gilbert lifted his head.
> "What ring is that?" he asked.
> Emmie started, and stared defiantly.
> "What, this? It's my engagement ring."
> "Mine", said Childe Rolande, with a sulky yelp. Whereupon he became nearly as red as the re-composed ruby.
> And immediately the frost settled down again, the padlocks snapped shut, and the solder went hard in the burning lid-joints of Walter George's heart. For a few seconds, Gilbert went to sleep, the cold air having numbed him. Walter George sat on the edge of the bed and looked over blackly at his toe-tips. Emmie tried to scheme, and almost got hold of the tail of a situation, when it evaded her again.[24]

Whereupon the narrator summarily dismisses his actors and there is, with a characteristic *coup de théâtre*, a change of scene. The writing is only superficially like Bennett's; Lawrence parodies Bennett's flair for the concrete one-line image of 'correlative' of a state of mind, then moves swiftly on to conclude his chapter in quite other ways (mostly telling his reader, if she is still there, about the 'scandalous' second volume where the cow has jumped over the moon and the dish ran away with the spoon: execrable puns also have their place in the carnival repertoire.

Switching the locale to Germany greatly enlarges the scope of the carnivalesque and the dialogic. Dialogue is now enriched by 'polymorphous' international misunderstandings and cultural confusions (what did that 'German lady' *really* think of the Japanese who pressed his legs against her knees? Is it true that she wanted to have his baby?); and the appearance of Joanna in the novel redoubles the sexual chanciness associated with carnivalisation, since she is, as I have said, as liberal with her sexual favours as Frieda apparently was in the early days of her relationship with

Lawrence. Nothing, literally, is sacred, since the Catholic ambiance also provides rich scope for blasphemy, a traditional component of the carnival. A mock sermon on spiritual uplift, for instance, follows a naked romp which itself comes hard upon statistical evidence of Noon's potency (three times in a quarter of an hour, no less), and in Chapter XXI there is a thoroughly tasteless and very funny disquisition upon the crucified Christ's INRI, glossed as old 'Inry' (Henry) 'selling joints'. A scatalogical element, part of the 'inversion' of the spiritual and the fleshly that carnival trades upon, is introduced in the form of an argument about divine 'afflatus', which prepares the way for a number of lavatorial episodes. Lawrence, through Frieda, has shed his Puritanism sufficiently to be able to celebrate 'the ancient pagan grossness, something Medieval and Roman even, in the brutality of the fair'.[25] In the 'metaphysical' debates between the soul and the body, the body looks set fair to win. Noon and Joanna make love in a ditch *à la* Crazy Jane, immediately after he has praised the lily not for its purity but for keeping its roots well down in the muck (a different angle on *Fleurs du Mal*). Lawrence quotes, and derides, Tolstoy on the tragedy of the bedroom; Life thrives, he says, upon the clash of opposites in marriage, and English literature, despite the fact that the English *do* take marriage seriously, has never been able to comprehend this.

But despite the euphoria, a certain amount of special pleading has entered the argument by this stage, as well as a self-justificatory tone. Joanna is, after all, a problem. Her occasional seduction of visitors does not seem to bother Noon too much; but there is precious little in his life apart from his woman (the references to his composing are very perfunctory). Chapter XIX is crucial: in it, his fascination with Joanna – there are times when he literally cannot take his eyes off her – is checked by her derision at what she sees as his pusillanimity. He is driven to insist that 'true, terrible marriage' is the real creation, 'not the accident of childbirth, but the miracle of man-birth and woman-birth' (we cannot forget how painful it was for Frieda to give up her children). We find Noon looking wistfully after the soldiers and the mowers; his own life 'did not unite him with mankind', and it is at this point that the genre of travelogue, hitherto present in uneasy tension with other genres, comes to dominate. It is not for nothing that Lawrence's narrator keeps reminding us that the world he is describing is a lost world.

Noon even writes to Emmie back in Woodhouse; and the journey begins to take on an edge of anxiety. Is the tragedy of the crucified Christ about to be played out again for real? St Paul tells us that God is not mocked.

The landscapes that are described more and more frequently as this novel moves towards its (unfinished) end are not in the least like those of either *Sons and Lovers* or *Women in Love*, except in a purely geographical sense. They do not accumulate symbolic resonances, beyond the opening up of a new sky to Noon. Above all, they do not serve as receptacles for displaced sexual energies, for we are to believe that the process of displacement has run its course. The shattering reality which Noon accepts with joy is the reality of female sexual desire, which even *Women in Love* had subordinated to an intricate critique of culture ('sublimation'). Joanna is a revelation; like Will on his honeymoon, but stripped of his Biblical 'apparatus', Noon feels all his inhibitions dropping away, at the liberating touch of a woman:

> So it is with man, gentle reader. There are worlds within worlds within worlds of unknown life and joy inside him. But every time, it needs a sort of cataclysm to get out of the old world into the new. It needs a very painful shedding of an old skin. It needs a fight with the matrix of the old era, a bitter struggle to the death with the old, warm, well-known mother of our days.

The liberation is nevertheless equivocal, even here. Gilbert welcomes the battle with the unknown Joanna; but Lawrence's delight at sloughing off the grime of England and playing fast and loose with Bennett's 'popular' fiction, fiction which held on tight to the known world and would shed none of its old skin, could not last. Even while he was revelling in his new freedom, Lawrence was embarking again upon his weary pursuit of chimerical satisfactions in a (largely illusory) world of prestige and influence that he would never enter. The novels of this period are sometimes called the novels of 'male power'. They ought to be called the novels of male impotence.

6

Living and Partly Living

Aaron's Rod, Kangaroo, and *The Plumed Serpent*

It may come as a surprise to find that Lawrence, even while celebrating (and justifying) his own sprightly livanting and rejoicing in Joanna's rich sexuality in *Mr Noon*, should at the same time have been weaving and unweaving another intricate narrative in which he imagined more comprehensive kinds of escape. Mr Noon, like Alvina, is 'liberated' for the time being from the more oppressive forms of family routine. But there are other nets cast, it seems, to trap the sensitive male soul. It is not just Midlands domesticity that must be outwitted, but the power of the Female as such. Linking fantasies of male self-sufficiency with new kinds of writerly freedom from narrative 'Law', Lawrence has produced in *Aaron's Rod* (1922) a heady synthesis of satirical fiction and the contingencies of travelogue, infusing the whole so deeply with fear and suspicion of women that in places it starts to look like the sort of 'gay' novel that *Women in Love*, from the evidence of the unpublished preface, might have become. Aaron's deepest relationship is with Rawdon, though it might be more accurate to say that the two men are one split hero,[1] and their contrasting feelings about marriage, and about the state of the world, reflect Lawrence's uneasy ambivalence. As with *Mr Noon* the protagonist is a peg to hang a narrative on, or a set of correlatives for shifting authorial positions, as well as being Modern Man in Search of a Soul (in the Bible the volatile 'dialogic' Aaron is contrasted with the powerful 'monologic' Moses of the Commandments). We have moved beyond the Waste Land of *Women in Love*, but in a shattered and unstable Europe the remnants of the cultural value system

('Law') are no longer efficacious. Lawrence's improvisatory vitality, ranging from liberating playfulness (cf. *The Lost Girl*) to frantic gesturing, is a positive response to this fact. What is more (and this sets the tone of succeeding novels and stories) English culture, and the English language, no longer have the hegemonic power and authority they had before the War. The capacity for experience has drained out of the Anglo-Saxon world faster, and more completely, than it has from the Mediterranean or more remote cultures (cf. Forster, though here again he seems parochial by Lawrence's side). Much of Lawrence's satire is directed at the representatives of Englishness, in one form or another: its snobbery, materialism, hypocrisy, and marionette-like rigidity. Towards the end of the decade, this abrasiveness is complemented by the search for a faith and a creed, emerging most resonantly in *The Plumed Serpent* and *Lady Chatterley's Lover*.

When Lawrence, with the dramatic, directionless, 'defamiliarising' style he developed during the 1920s[2] to match his increasing sense of the collapse of narrative authority, describes Angus, in Chapter fifteen, 'pitching camp in the midst of civilisation', the paradox conveys the essence of this novel. Whereas Mr Noon, and Alvina, were like vortices through which the narrative energies were discharged, Aaron is a half-formed creature, acted upon and unable to resist, charmed by the men (and occasional women) he meets, and finding aspects of himself reflected in their often curious behaviour, but uncertain how to approach them, a fugitive, and a spectator at life's play. Ill-equipped and insecure without his wife, he consoles himself with his 'rod' (his flute), indulging in a kind of onanistic melancholy that is briefly interrupted by his affair with the Marchesa. As with Lawrence's other travel writings of this period, ecstatic responses to the 'otherness' of place alternate with neurasthenic encounters with the dark side of the psyche: the Oedipal symptoms of the earlier novels are still vestigially present. The opening chapters of the novel are drawn with remarkable exactness and economy, and seem to have left a strong impress on the work of David Storey, whom I have already described as Lawrence's most worthy successor.[3] They evoke the oppressiveness in English domesticity that forces Aaron to take flight (Sheila Macleod censures Lawrence for disregarding the fate of his wife Lottie and the children) and are loosely paralleled later in the episodes in Chapters sixteen and eighteen where Aaron catches a guilty glimpse of 'freedom' with the Marchesa, who is similarly impatient with the 'chains of necessity' imposed by marriage, and whose husband delivers a mysogynistic, and strangely modern, diatribe on marriage that cuts through English hypocrisies (or idealism?) and is brilliantly, unpleasantly, echoed by Argyle, another 'damaged' character. Aaron's flight from the responsibilities of marriage is correlated with a kind of authorial striking out into the narrative wilderness. Like Aaron surveying his home from the vantage point of the garden shed, trying to decode the 'hieroglyph' of his native countryside, Lawrence wilfully estranges himself from his narrative, creating self-contained satirical or quasi-satirical episodes strung together randomly by a motif or two (the blue ball of Chapter one that arbitrarily codes the destruction of the father's authority, or the candle motif of Chapter three which serves, *faute de mieux*, to link up a narrative sequence). Christmas is the kind of shared family event that can admirably point up disaffection.

On the ideological plane we see a similar lack of commitment. Chapter six, called 'Talk', is, like others, a lively compendium of vague politicising and peculiarly English snobbery, with Aaron already functioning as the drifting and arbitrary focal point of an endless, apparently pointless, dialogue. There is a feeling that real power lies elsewhere, if one could only locate it, and that one's life is determined from hidden, or secret, places: a notion which may reflect, on one level, the trauma of war and post-war political paranoia, but which also (as the growing spiritual awareness of these novels, and of *Lady Chatterley's Lover* gradually makes manifest) expresses a religious sense of being in the presence of a higher authority. This consorts oddly with the air of malice and mockery that hangs over the book, as it does over the masterly short novel *St Mawr*, written a few years later, whose theme is how society lives by mutual 'undermining'. Aaron's 'low water mark' does indeed come in the chapter of that title (Chapter nine) in which, like Lawrence in this period, he shows symptoms of clinical depression, and is rescued and supported by Rawdon Lilly, his *doppelgänger*, after trying to drown his sorrows. The full force of the chapter's title comes out in the strange relationship that grows between the two men, based upon a homoerotic intimacy of touch in the 'secret places', and the beginnings of the long debate about the relationship of authority to power. The communing of the male 'dark gods' represents an extreme reaction against 'the Female'. At the other end of the spectrum, Lord and Lady Franks act out their gracious charade of being a ruling élite, which is punctuated by comic opera fantasies of the Italian peasants rising and dispossessing them of their splendid home.

The unreality both of the Franks ménage and the imagined threat to it prompts Aaron to reflect back upon his own home and marriage, as possibly more real because less given to game-playing; his bitter but horribly truthful meditations seem to reflect the darker side of Lawrence's marriage at the time. Combining novelistic and speculative modes of writing in the free-wheeling manner typical of this 'group' of novels, Lawrence reaffirms Birkin's creed of separateness ('star-polarity'); if life is, as Aaron claims (in the spirit of the *Study of Thomas Hardy*) not a conservation of energy, but an expenditure of energy, no marriage can work which does not respect this principle. The basic law for men and for women is 'give thyself, but give thyself not away'. Lawrence's seminal essay on Edgar Allan Poe is echoed in the argument that it is the death of any relationship when it degenerates 'into a sort of slime and merge'. Fulfilment can only come through singleness and the kind of changefulness that Birkin celebrated: 'never to be saddled with an idée fixe'; but the insistence on separateness has become so extreme that it looks as if, for this novel at least, marriage is irrelevant. In the swirl of conversation, two 'structural' points emerge. One is made by musical analogy: a promotion of Stravinsky over Beethoven, since the former does not fasten you down to 'depths', seems to correspond to Lawrence's experimental improvised narrative, an art of surfaces, of 'bricolage',[4] to some extent of pastiche, which despite its fierce polemic, has indefinitely postponed any 'totalising' vision or authoritative statement. Linked to this point is another: the power struggle of the tense, alcohol-charged conversation comes to rest for a moment on a phrase from an anthem:

His eye is on the sparrow
So I know he watches me.

The mishearing of these lines as 'his eye is on the spy-hole' focuses the estrangement of Lawrence's narrative *vis-à-vis* authorial omniscience: the problem, in fact, of power and authority that the

novel keeps coming back to in one form or another, but never fully
engages with.

Actual political violence is never far away, of course. Italy is
volatile, on the eve of the Fascist takeover. Shots are fired in
Chapter fourteen, and a bomb outrage more or less terminates the
action of the novel by destroying Aaron's rod (which had no time
properly to blossom). The sardonic Angus is a casualty of war, a
victim of shell-shock, half 'pre-war baby' and half 'shattered old
man' (his own phrases) who defends himself against further hurt
by saying of the man who fell from the window, 'It's one of the
funniest things I ever did see. I saw nothing quite like it, even in the
war';[5] a desperate defensiveness which is also part of Aaron's
make-up. There is a kind of mental violence, too; instant theories
fly back and forth within and around the *huis clos* situations,
emphasising the difficulty of finding a way forward. The splendid
chapter called 'Florence'[6] has the representative 'superficiality' of
the whole novel, with its bitty, fragmented exchanges disrupted by
inner violence, and the resistance to depth mentioned above.
Around the great Renaissance statues spirals an argument about
the essentially male creative quality of gratuitousness (cf. the *Study
of Thomas Hardy*)[7] though this is already turning sour both outside
and inside the fiction, and giving way to something more sinister, a
political formula for the annexation of authority by power which
many readers have found troubling. Nowhere does Lawrence
support the Fascists; indeed in at least two places (*Sea and Sardinia*
and *The Plumed Serpent*) he condemns them; but some of his views,
like those of the Futurists, could be assimilated to Fascist ideology.

It is ironic that it should be the Marchesa who articulates the
philosophy of contingency by which Aaron seeks to live. She has
chosen to remain in a loveless marriage, from which Aaron is
powerless to deliver her; while Aaron, the renegade, is too unsure
of himself, especially where she is concerned, to know where his
life is taking him. His own first reaction is defensive, to safeguard
his phallic instrument (to the extent of pretending he has not
brought it: 'I didn't want to arrive with a little bag'). As the
relationship between the two develops, so the spurious philosophy
of 'male power' begins to emerge. In assessing it we ought to
register the defensiveness of such propositions as (apropos of
Aaron) 'newly flushed with his own male super-power'; he is, after
all, a tentative and inept lover, on the run from his own woman,

and this fact makes a difference to how we read (for example),

> His manhood, or rather his maleness, rose powerfully in him, in
> a sort of mastery. He felt his own power, he felt suddenly his own
> virile title to strength and reward.[8]

Guilt and depression rapidly follow:

> His brain felt withered, his mind had only one of its many-
> sighted eyes left open and unscorched. So many of the eyes of his
> mind were scorched now and sightless.[9]

It is not surprising that the novel ends with Lilly urging a
disengagement from the 'love-mode'.

Lawrence evidently felt that the rather impromptu themes of
Aaron's Rod needed to be developed more fully. *Kangaroo* followed
in 1923, and it is even more rapid, improvised, and open ended;
the impact of the War is also more explicit. Marriage, however, is
still seen in this novel as a (precarious) force for cohesion. *Aaron's
Rod* offered the proposition that 'Much that is life has passed away
from men, leaving us all mere bits'. *Kangaroo* has a chapter called
'Bits' (as well as one directly concerned with the nightmare of the
War) in which the violent destruction of a culture, and the inner
sense of loss and meaninglessness which Eliot called the 'dissociation of sensibility', are charted in abrasive collage-like clippings
from the press. But *Kangaroo* is also more overtly political than
Aaron's Rod, involving a strange flirtation with Australian nationalism. Australia, a gift to Lawrence's spikey style of travelogue,
provided the basis for a book which its author accurately described
as a 'funny sort of novel where nothing happens and such a lot of
things *should* happen: scene Australia'.[10] But it also precipitated an
anguished fable of modern marriage, running head-on at the
issues that *Aaron's Rod* dodged. This is the novel in which Lawrence
and Frieda appear most unequivocally as themselves; indeed, the
whole story has something of the air of a celebrity tour, except that
Lovat Somers is not much of a celebrity, and the 'tour' is largely a
struggle with a recalcitrant landscape and a 'democracy' ('the little
square bungalows dot-to-dot, close together and yet apart, like
modern democracy')[11] which scrambles the cultural codes in fascinating but bewildering ways ('Torestin' is not, it turns out, a

Russian word). The quest for a new order has become more urgent than in *Aaron's Rod*, and is matched by the stridency of Australian politics.

Just as the desert is a place of prophecy, so the empty Australian landscape, by virtue of its cultural poverty, is rich in possibilities. Lawrence's descriptive writing, for example, blossoms exotically as it meditates upon an inhuman landscape which seems to speak to the post-war world in its own language:

> The previous world! – the world of the coal age. The lonely, lonely world that had waited, it seemed, since the coal age. These ancient flat-topped tree-ferns, these towsled palms like mops. What was the good of trying to be an alert conscious man here? You couldn't. Drift, drift into a sort of obscurity, backwards into a nameless past, hoary as the country is hoary. Strange old feelings wake in the soul: old, non-human feelings. And an old, old indifference, like a torpor invades the spirit. An old, saurian torpor. Who wins? There was the land sprinkled with dwellings as with granulated sugar. There was a black smoke of steamers on the high pale sea, and a whiteness of steam from a colliery among the dull trees. Was the land awake? Would the people waken this ancient land, or would the land put them to sleep, drift them back into the torpid semi-consciousness of the world of the twilight.[12]

The collocation of registers here, the collage of 'bits', is remarkable (it is, of course, a staple of the novel: the extraordinary chapter called 'Volcanic Evidence' pushes a description of jelly-fish hard up against excerpts from a letter from home and follows it with bits from the *Sydney Telegraph*). The narrator struggles to situate himself in relation to a reality which lies outside his experience, but which, from its very 'previousnessness' (Baudelaire's 'la vie antér-ieure') chimes in with a range of associations from the Old World (including coal, a favourite Lawrence metaphor of the uncon-scious). The complex relation between speaker and listener is characteristic; there is a rhetoric of persuasion, even an assertive-ness ('You couldn't'), but the whole is in a kind of inverted commas, since 'drift' is far from being Lawrence's position, or, indeed, the movement of the fiction. There is a problem of 'focalisation',[13] characteristic of Lawrence's later fiction, maybe even including

Women in Love (the absence of a final question mark gives the last sentence here a tentative provisionality, rather than a real interrogative force).

Just as the imagery of this kind of writing harks back to the Old World and bears out Somers' early impression that Australia is 'the other end of English and American business', so the commentary on marriage, which counterpoints the commentary on power, keeps returning to the European nightmare which Australia, far from escaping by being so 'far away', has inherited the consequences of, with very little by way of defence ('It was in 1915 the old world ended').[14] Small wonder that Harriet and Lovat should be 'at sea in marriage', in the brilliant improvised fable of that title,[15] when there is so little else to have survived the crash, apart from marriage, to offer an image of one's own experience that is not all 'bits'. But small wonder also that political life is so raw and violent, oscillating as it does between the extremes of Nationalism (with strongly Christian and mysogynist overtones) and Socialism. The Kangaroo rhetoric, which might justly be accused of 'aestheticising politics',[16] chimes in with the fantasies of many of the major Modernist writers about 'things falling apart'.

Here is a philosophy of the chosen few, permeated with beguiling adolescent sentiments ('Most people are dead, and scurrying and talking in the sleep of death') and it is not surprising that for some readers this recalls Fascism; but without indulging in special pleading we can make the point that Australian nationalism by no means has the last word in the novel. Somers and Kangaroo fall out, Kangaroo is killed, the political millenium fails to materialise, and the 'great mistake' that Australia has so far managed to avoid is staved off.[17] Nothing much is resolved, but the failure of ideology leaves us with the equivocal image of the spoiled/unspoiled Australian landscape, illuminating in 'bits' the devastation of the modern European mind. That and the bleak landscape of Lawrence's marriage, which is perhaps, as I have suggested, what the whole novel was really about at another, displaced, level:

Harriet and he? It was time they both agreed that nothing has any meaning. Meaning is a dead letter when a man has no soul. And speech is like a volley of dead leaves and dust, stifling the air. Human beings should learn to make weird, wordless cries like the animals, and cast off the clutter of words.[18]

The Plumed Serpent (1926) tries to 'cast off the clutter of words' (Lawrence had taken up painting again) in its ritual, gestural pursuit of the 'strange gods', and goes through odd contortions in its efforts to recoup the ground lost as Frieda's interest in other men pushed the ailing Lawrence deeper and deeper into his corner. An exotic landscape, a renascent cult of masculinity, an obligingly world-weary female looking for something a little different: on the face of it, all the ingredients of the bodice-ripping romance are flaunted in this novel. It may indeed be the case, as Brian Finney has suggested, that Lawrence consistently parodies romance forms and conventions in his later fiction;[19] and this in turn may link up with his preoccupation, everywhere after *Women in Love*, with the dynamics of 'popular' writing (it depends how you construct 'the people', as Lawrence well knew). *Lady Chatterly's Lover* certainly makes most sense read as a romance, or as a version of pastoral. But the most powerful element in *The Plumed Serpent*, as in *Lady Chatterley's Lover*, is the quest motif, and despite the exoticism of the travel writing in the book we are bound to feel that we are coming closer and closer to home and perhaps to a final point of rest: it was not only Kate, but Lawrence, who celebrated a 'Fortieth Birthday' in 1925. *Lady Chatterley's Lover* begins, 'ours is essentially a tragic age', and *The Plumed Serpent* foreshadows it in struggling to define this tragedy in relation to the political violence of our age and the radical confusion of power and authority in a dying culture (a confusion in Lawrence's own mind too).

The novel also tries harder than *Aaron's Rod* or *Kangaroo* to make a positive statement of faith. Mexico serves Lawrence's didactic purposes better than either Italy or Australia. Its landscape is as violent as its political history, and in the period in which Lawrence was writing it had already become a stamping ground for the revolutionary ideologies emergent in Europe. Kate, who is Irish, finds that it reminds her of Ireland, in the sense that the oppressive proximity of a more powerful nation has both distorted the political history of the country and generated a kind of imaginative, or spiritual, energy that remains to be trapped. The 'expatriate' theme that runs through *Aaron's Rod* and *Kangaroo* has thus acquired a new edge. Now we have to reckon not just with a scatter of generally rather ridiculous Anglo-Saxons serving as sounding boards for political and emotional processes; we must take on board as well the deep-seated violence of a country in a state of permanent revolt against an infinitely more powerful neighbour, the USA, with a culture and a language set fair to colonise the world. The threatening presence of the United States in Mexican life is hinted at from the opening pages of the novel, in the shape of Americans like Villiers who, as good tourists, take a voyeuristic pleasure in violence. The bullfight economically prepares us for later, more disturbing instances of violence indigenous to the land, and thence to the human sacrifice of the plumed serpent cult, presented as being rather more meaningful than being cut to pieces by brigands. Thus by a circuitous route a specific English anxiety (about engulfment by the United States, mass civilisation, and 'capitalism') finds expression both on a global scale and in the particular terms of a keen sense of the fragile identity of one person, Kate, who has reached an age where she feels the need to evaluate her life so far and reaffirm her hold on 'experience'. This urge becomes more powerful as death approaches; it is her last chance. Mexico's dark gods thrill Lawrence partly because, far more than Christ, they rule over the kingdom of the dead, and speak directly to a man who must have felt that his days were numbered. Like Yeats setting sail for Byzantium, Lawrence has found in Mexico, or been able to invent, a culture with a potential for living by spiritual, or metaphysical, values, and an impersonality that restores meaning to the personal, time-bound struggle of the artist.

It is a truism that in our time political life has become a show, a mass spectator sport, thanks mainly to television. For Lawrence, this process started with Lloyd George, and the 'revolutionary' dictators, Lenin, Mussolini, Hitler, Stalin etc., developed it, exploiting new information technologies. In *The Plumed Serpent* the theatricality of politics is taken for granted, and we (the privileged spectators of Kate's passionate involvement) are taken backstage to observe the construction of rather operatic scenarios of political power out of a collage of fragments of nonconformist hymns, Victorian medievalism (Morris' *News from Nowhere* and Carlyle's *Past and Present*), newspaper 'bits' (as in *Kangaroo*), Hollywood romances, and Nietzsche's *Zarathustra*, among other things. The 'revolutionary' prophets of Quetzalcoatl, Don Ramon and Don Cipriano, though superficially modelled on the European tyrants, are nevertheless motivated in their careers by something other than a sheer desire for power. Their manipulations and connivances are to be understood as the necessary preparations for introducing a liturgy that will make it possible to approach spiritual truth in a fallen age. Don Ramon, for instance, has been accused of giving the Fascist salute; actually it is not very different from the Yoga salute to the sun; one makes of that what one will. The end justifying the means? There may well be some moral confusion in the politics of the novel, symptomatic of our tragic age, but in point of fact we never depart very far from Christian values. The religion of Quetzalcoatl depends heavily on rewrites (not even very unorthodox ones) of the Bible and the Book of Common Prayer. The radical appeal and novelty of the 'strange gods' is tempered by the fact that the cult of Quetzalcoatl, in scenes reminiscent of Eisenstein, depends upon blasphemy (i.e. the systematic denigration of Christ) and, as Harry T. Moore has pointed out, the Hymns are often free paraphrases of the nonconformist hymns of Lawrence's youth. We are actually very close to the world of *A Propos of Lady Chatterley's Lover*, where Catholic liturgy is praised for its power of mediation between man and the unknown, and for a kind of ancestor-worship, or preservation of the race-memory.

Kate, likewise, prefigures Connie Chatterley. She has buried her husband: 'Joachim has gone into eternity in death, and she had crossed with him into a certain eternity of life'. It is this Byzantine detachment from passion and transformation into a different, and purer, mode of being that she seeks through her encounters with a land in the throes of rejecting European and American humanism and the sinister commercial values that follow in its wake. Her isolation is stressed, especially after she has dropped the feeble Villiers, but so is her fierce determination to discover the real core of herself. It is easy to deride Lawrence for showing this discovery taking place (as in *Lady Chatterley's Lover*) through copulation with a charismatic man, or to write the whole thing off as compensatory fantasy: and I have suggested that Lawrence's ego needed a boost at the time (the tense relationship between Ramon and his wife Carlota has an autobiographical dimension). But as in *Lady Chatterley's Lover*, the emphasis lies on the power of spiritual renewal as much as it does on sex, let alone the dominant male. Both novels insist that sex is properly to be thought of as sacramental, issuing from, and validated by, impersonal presences, which are what make it healing rather than wounding. It is only through the impersonal that the personal can be restored: Lawrence's 'anti-humanism' (the term has an obvious validity) never loses sight of the fact that life goes on in and between *individuals*.[20] The latter part of the novel is taken up with descriptions of the rituals of the Plumed Serpent, and although these are too long, and uncomfortably reminiscent of the Natcha Kee Tawara 'rites of passage' in *The Lost Girl* (which are, after all, meant to be a bit absurd), Lawrence's commitment irradiates them. It is hard, in our time, and especially in our Protestant culture, or what is left of it, to imagine how 'ritual' might mean anything other than a tedious, probably reactionary, social form; but Lawrence's experience (and his sense of the enormous difficulty of *possessing* one's own experience) had convinced him of the need to renew life from deep 'racial'[21] psychic sources which can be best expressed through dramatic rituals: like Artaud,[22] Eliot, and others of his generation, as well as the great psychoanalysts who locate the sources and structures of consciousness in ritual and myth. Kate is both fascinated and repelled; but it is important to insist that what she discovers in the untapped potential of Mexico is, first and foremost, herself; the justification of the rituals resides in the extent to which the Morning Star (the dimension of the impersonal) can meet the needs of the middle-aged protagonist. This may sound like an odd way of introducing *Lady Chatterley's Lover*, but Lawrence's last novel is, I believe, especially in its third (final) form, the necessary culmination of the arguments of *The Plumed Serpent*.

7

Naming of Parts
Lady Chatterley's Lover

Lady Chatterley's Lover has an unusual publishing history, to put it mildly. Printed in Florence by Pino Orioli (being unpublishable in prudish England) it was not available in its entirety in this country until after the infamous trial of Penguin Books in 1960. At the trial, those witnesses who cared about the book's literary merits defended it as a statement about married love. Actually, it is (of course) about adultery, that mainstay of nineteenth-century realism, which it treats in a manner, and from an angle, significantly different from that of the great classics. One way of reading Lawrence's novel, indeed, is to see it as the author's riposte to Tolstoy's *Anna Karenina*, a book which he took against for obvious personal reasons.[1] It is also a reaction against the 'pornography' of the nineteenth-century classics, which Lawrence was among the first commentators of either sex to identify.[2] Any way of reading it will have to take account of the range of (sometimes contradictory) things it tries to do. In several important respects it is not, nor is it meant to be, realistic. It belongs with the revived quest literature of Modernism (I have already mentioned 'The Waste Land') and draws extensively upon folklore and mythology (of the rather literary *Golden Bough* type). 'Romance' describes it rather well (shades of Jessie Weston).[3] Like other Lawrence novels, it is accompanied by its own 'metaphysics' in the shape of an essay offering to tell you how to read it, entitled *A Propos of Lady Chatterley's Lover*. This fascinating document is partly concerned with the absurdities of censorship (on which subject Lawrence manages to keep fairly cool and sensible). For the rest, it goes in two contradictory directions simultaneously, perhaps like the novel. One might be described as 'mental hygiene': Lawrence wants to help us to 'think sex' openly and without embarrassment. To this end a range of forbidden words are redeployed, in the hope that they will be made available for immediate use (Lawrence's faith in the power of literature here is remarkable, and wholly characteristic). But simultaneously with this there is another, more profound, purpose. This might be understood in terms of the endeavour to construct a sacral space around the sexual act. This evidently has nothing to do with demystifying; quite the reverse, since it is Lawrence's passionate conviction that censoring sex, and the language of sex, has led to a reaction in the form of the cheapening and vulgarising of a sacred mystery: the creation of the 'dirty little secret'. Where Freud suggests that sublimation is civilisation's 'answer' to a sexual drive which can never be fully satisfied, Lawrence tells us that our sexual experience is close to the sources of our religious sense of mystery and of life. To call it a 'drive' is just another way of cheapening it. As I suggested in my previous chapter, Lawrence was moving in his last years towards a renewed sense of the reality of the transcendental within the symbolic order of our culture, that which the unweaving of the rainbow had undermined. His use of the word 'phallic' has been misunderstood, and perhaps the choice of term was unfortunate. The phallic, as he understands it, has nothing to do with Freud's stage of development; nor is it synonymous with the use of the word in feminist theory. The phallic is the domain of the Morning Star; it may be experienced in chastity as well as in sexual intercourse; it does not suggest male dominance; it does suggest that sexual experience transcends self.

And here, indeed, is the essential problem. *Lady Chatterley's Lover* would not have given half so much offence if, like Frank Harris's autobiography,[4] it had simply been the more or less 'forbidden' journal of a profligate, and the sexual encounters had not amounted to much more than a naming of parts, as with Harris. Lawrence's novel is intensely personal, in more senses than one. Gone are the elaborate scenarios of the three preceding novels; and the fierce political debate embarked upon in those novels, which is still highly significant, is brought home to where it started from, in a recognisable English Romantic tradition. The novel is 'through-composed'[5] in the form of a sustained lyrical threnody for contemporary civilisation, weaving together motifs of life and of death, rather than a synthetic composite of 'bits'. Moreover, it sustains a delicate 'I – thou' relationship between the protagonists, never lapsing into mere instrumentality,[6] even when the varieties of sexual experience described include some that might be called perverse, or sexual parts are referred to impersonally. In relation to Lawrence's life and his development as a writer, it is not only his swan-song but a kind of completion of the circle (knowing the place for the first time).[7] It is a remarkable reaffirmation, in the midst of unbearable pain, of the enduring power of hope and the human imagination. In terms of Lawrence's own experience, and his situation towards the end of the 1920s, it fuses together a number of very personal motifs in fascinating ways, and the characters seem to represent contrary aspects of one whole.

From one angle, the gamekeeper protagonist Mellors evidently serves Lawrence as a vehicle for his sexual fantasies, and his thwarted need to love and cherish a woman, perhaps in response to Frieda's growing restlessness in their marriage (and he even catches Lawrence's cough).[8] Bertha perhaps represents sexual demands that the ailing Lawrence could not meet, and her portrayal in the novel is certainly degrading. But Lawrence is also Sir Clifford, the Fisher King presiding over the Waste Land, disabled by modern civilisation, knowing that the land will not bloom again until the Sleeping Beauty presents it with an heir (the Lawrences had no children of their own). Sir Clifford needs, like Lawrence, a lot of mothering. As a writer, he 'leaves everything in bits at the end'[9] and is cultivating a humorous, malicious, gossipy style – and although this is never the *whole* of what Lawrence does in any given work, it is a major part of what has gone into the three previous novels, as well as *St. Mawr*, all of which work in terms of 'bits'. Mellors, of course, 'transgresses' the boundaries betwen codes, as did Lawrence, in several ways.[10] But it is Clifford who writes; and there is a characteristic interplay between written and oral modes in the novel as it gropes towards the 'roots' of language (Anglo-Saxon or Celtic) and tries, like 'The Waste Land', to identify those which clutch out of the stony rubbish.

All writing is crippled, in our time, by its divorce from the grain and rhythms of the voice and from bodily rhythms and gestures (properties which the Modernist writer strives to restore; Pound, for instance, had an intricate terminology for this). Maybe Michaelis's brief hole-and-corner affair with Connie has something to do with Lawrence's half-hearted infidelity with Dorothy Brett; at all events, this is another variety of sexual experience which Lawrence, who had scarcely experienced it at first hand, is trying to bring out of the closet, and help us to accept as part of our lives, with sadness, perhaps, but without rancour or regret. As I have said, the novel celebrates both marriage and adultery, seeing them as complementary (as they obviously are, though the anathematising of the adulteress in nineteenth-century fiction might lead us to believe otherwise). Lawrence, like Malinowski in his classic work on the family,[11] marvels at the human capacity for lasting tenderness towards a sexual partner (love is one of the 'great words' that have been 'cancelled') and reaffirms marriage as an institution that will and must survive as the nucleus of any kind of social hope. Malinowski tells us that this has always been the case, and that anthropological accounts of alternative structures of kinship are misleading or just plain wrong.[12] Meanwhile, the battle of the sexes goes on: while the men enjoy 'the old free-masonry of male sensuality'[13] the women (decidedly in the minority) keep life's wheels turning. Lawrence suggests that it has always been like this, and always will be; but in the act of love, man and woman are equal, and both are subject to the influence of another, greater, 'presence'.

Here we enter the realm of the massive, melancholy 'critique of culture' which this novel offers, and which has been so influential (and provoked so much resentment). Central to it is a conservative thesis about language, which I have already compared to Eliot's: that hidden in the 'secret places' is a true and incorruptible language of feeling which has been lost or defiled by modern civilisation; an ideal conjunction of the signifier with the signified whereby we can/could once say (or write) what we feel/felt with no shadow (to use Eliot's word) coming between. This is one reading of 'coming off together' and of Iacchos, the phallos, which is 'pure god-servant to the woman', and it is a deep-seated Modernist mythology. Thus we have Connie, rather like Joyce's Stephen Dedalus, ruminating on how words can change their meanings, or how meaning can drain out of them (love, joy, happiness, home, mother, father, husband). Writers like Sir Clifford, or Michaelis, presenting their cerebral 'bits' to the bitch-goddess of success, have helped to erode meaning, but Connie, being a woman, is unimpressed by their material success (Michaelis, suggestively enough, has the habit of working his hands in his pockets, and his inadequate sexual performance is accompanied by attempts to blame her. He is another representative of the abstract demon of writing with its negative power and vindictiveness). Another major component of 'coming together' is the symbolic reunion of the sundered classes; Lawrence lived all his life with a perception of the 'split' in his own being between middle class and working class. Here again, the critique of language is significant, since it is the 'four letter words', thought of somehow as 'working class', that will now have to serve us, indeed may serve us better than any other, to speak of those vital centres of experience which have been tabooed and travestied but which hold the key to the future. Mellors's version of the 'naming of parts' is a mixture of magical ritual and puppet-play (featuring our old friends John Thomas and Lady Jane), with the carnival inversion of reason and the 'lower' function corresponding to the inversion of social hierarchies (the 'working man' – though actually he is not – gives the lead to the lady of the manor). In a kind of amalgam of the Raggle-Taggle Gypsies and Strindberg's *Miss Julie*, Mellors becomes the master of the revels; a part he is well qualified to play because of his double identity, as army officer and man of the people, and his ambivalent position (is the 'law' he enforces natural or cultural? has the gamekeeper turned poacher?). Another 'coming together' is that of Father and Son, our age's great Act of Atonement for which Joyce struggled throughout his writing life. In a closing of the hermeneutic circle, Mellors/Morel is both father and son: the son as he *ought* to have been ('si vieillesse pouvait, si jeunesse savait'). It is easy to deride the way Mellors 'gives' Connie back her own body, as if she had not 'possessed' it herself from birth; and one sympathises with feminists who find all this pretty arrogant or even insulting. There are echoes of Paul Morel 'teaching' Baudelaire's poetry to Miriam. But provided one can accept sex as therapy, and believe that there are sexual encounters, in or out of wedlock, that are healing, and others that are violations, it should not be difficult to accept that Western man, and woman, *have* lost touch with themselves, and each other, as the proliferation of 'alternative' philosophies and therapies in our time demonstrates, and that a cure for Connie's depression – very accurately diagnosed and described – might well be a relationship with a man who respects her in body and in soul.

Compared with the three novels that precede it, *Lady Chatterley* is, despite the fact that it is working in two directions at once, stylistically coherent, and fully worked out imaginatively. One

dimension of this is the fact that the 'metaphysics' are much better
integrated than they are in the 'political' novels, and have been
brought into line once again with the 'physics' of writing, the 'body'
of the text, in a very special way. Yeats recognised this better than
any other of Lawrence's contemporaries, and in one, very Yeatsian,
pronouncement, summed up most of what holds the novel
together as a particular 'mood' or 'ambiance' (which is indeed
absolutely crucial):

> These two lovers, the gamekeeper and his employer's wife,
> each separated from their class by their love and fate, are
> poignant in their loneliness; the coarse language of the one
> accepted by both becomes a forlorn poetry, uniting their soli-
> tudes, something ancient, humble, and terrible.[14]

Yeats, connoisseur of impossibilities, knew very well how love and
fate could be at odds in ways Romeo and Juliet had never dreamed
of; 'employer's wife' is nice, and perhaps only Yeats could have got
away with it. Most interesting, however, is that allusion to the
'forlornness' of the 'poetry' (which is also the forlorn condition of
the protagonists, and of the modern world). Everything that
happens in the novel needs to be seen in relation to the tragic
backdrop of European civilisation destroying itself, so that Connie
and Mellors' 'union in solitude' is that much more rare, precious,
and vulnerable – 'we are a pair of battered warriors'[15] – and what it
promises is new life: not just for the lovers, but in the form of a
child.

In the emergent Europe of the dictators it must have been
harder and harder to believe in the future of civilised personal
relations like Mellors' and Connie's. The decay of the English
gentry (demolition of Shipley Hall, etc.) is not something to rejoice
in, either, since it is not much more than another symptom of the
power of a growing technocratic élite (David Storey does this theme
well in *Radcliffe*). The men are all damaged, even when, like
Tommy Dukes, they have charm, intelligence, and forthrightness,
so that there is very little chance of them rediscovering those
sources of vitality they have lost (Dukes 'like(s) women better than
men; they are braver, and one can be more frank with them.').
Connie has to allay Mellors' fears for the future; the novel is also
permeated by a middle-aged regret for the past, as Connie's rather
unfulfilled youth is evoked, and Mellors' unhappy marriage;

Connie's 'unspeakable depression' is by no means synonymous with sexual frustration (as the Sylvia Kristel film, intelligently scripted though it was, would have us believe.)[16] And yet the ability to affirm continuity and the future remains a profound human need.

As Yeats saw, and as he tells us obsessively in his own late poetry, love's mansion is situated in the place of excrement: the 'river of Life and the river of Dissolution' flow side by side.[17] The strongest theme in the novel is that of 'fuck(ing) a flame into being', and that flame, the new life made by sex, is specifically equated with a child. From the time of Connie's earliest visits to the gamekeeper's hut, when she weeps over the pheasant chicks, it is apparent that her life will not make sense to her until she has a child, and that Lawrence represents her liaison with the man, with scrupulous verisimilitude, as contracted primarily for that purpose (it has indubitably affected the rather partial accounts of female orgasm in the novel, for example, since from the book's other very circumstantial descriptions of sexual activity it is quite clear that Lawrence was not ignorant of the anatomical facts). I do not think that Lawrence finds space anywhere else in his fiction for anything like this affirmation of a woman's deep need to give birth, though he had doubtless come to feel the pathos of the childlessness of his own marriage; and the theme is completely integrated. It is 'childlessness' as a tragic theme, extending beyond the individual towards questions of faith and the future of society, that colours much of the highly charged negative writing which has traditionally been approvingly singled out from the body of the novel as a major statement of Lawrence's critique of contemporary civilisation:[18]

> The car ploughed uphill through the long squalid straggle of Tevershall, the blackened brick dwellings, the black slate roofs glistening their sharp edges, the mud black with coal-dust, the pavements wet and black. . . .

In the over-insistence, and the repetitions reminiscent of Dickens's *Hard Times*, this writing is not so much a critique of the aftermath of industrialism as an explosion of pent-up emotion in a familiar Lawrencian vein. The outrage obviously exceeds its object; why should anyone object, after all, to goods being available in the shops? –

> The stacks of soap in the grocers' shops, the rhubarb and lemons in the greengrocers! the awful hats in the milliners!

and so on; down to the school buildings, and the girls singing a 'sweet children's song'. The stridency of the writing may be better understood if we realise as fully as possible that it is written from Connie's point of view, and that it expresses her deathly sense of oppression. In her capacity as Persephone/Demeter, Connie belongs both to death and to life, to the Waste Land and to what lies beyond it. Lawrence rarely employs Free Indirect Discourse, or anything that might properly be called this; but he frequently writes from a narrative position situated, with a degree of mobility, somewhere in between the standpoint of a character and that of an external (and rather forceful) omniscient author, leaving the reader to find his or her bearings in relation to what is said, and to decide who speaks through whom, and to what end. However, this bitterly 'apocalyptic' vision of hats and lemons is the necessary negative dimension of the 'redemptive' vision of Persephone/ Connie liberated from the underworld. The sterility of the Tevershall landscape indubitably resides in the tragic loss and desire through which it is refracted, and the gritty details of the passage itself do not add up to an adequate correlative of these. Nor do I think it is a coincidence that the last extended reference in the passage is to the singing of schoolchildren. 'Yet she was wanting a baby, and an heir to Wragby.'[19] Yes, indeed, she was, though in her symbolic role it is not just Wragby that seeks to be reborn through her, but England.

Tragedy, said Lawrence, ought to be a great kick at misery.[20] On this Nietzschean view,[21] in order to 'take our age tragically' (in the spirit of the novel's opening) we need imaginative forms that will cathect the pent-up violence, grief and horror of what we experience day by day; especially we English, heirs to the post-industrial waste land and its monstrous class system. Mellors plays halfheartedly with ideas of communal frolics borrowed from William Morris,[22] but these are the residual musings of a lonely man, left over, as it were, from the 'political' novels. When it comes to defining what may be possible by way of overcoming the processes of alienation specific to our culture, Yeats's unusual plural 'solitudes' is very apposite, since the tragic aesthetic of the novel (this or another) seeks precisely to bring together *individuals* without any loss of self, and with a respect for the social realities of their existence, and to explore through the interaction of individuals something that can otherwise be found only in religion, myth and folklore, which the novel translates into modern terms. Lawrence had no use for the word 'erotic', it seems, and yet this novel links ideas of sex, transcendence, and death very much in the manner of Georges Bataille's *Eroticism*, and *Literature and Evil* (which owe a lot to Nietzsche). For Bataille, acts of transgression affirm 'continuity', the breaking of the boundaries of the self in sex and in death, surrender. Lawrence, defying Freud, has deliberately and outrageously assimilated nature to culture, in his designation of sex (lovemaking) as 'fucking'.

The transgression of taboos begins with the special use Lawrence makes of the masculine genre of the smoking-room story near the beginning of the novel, wherein Dukes, May and the others begin to name the unnameable, and it carries on into the 'transgressive' relationship of Connie and Mellors, with their enforced solitude and secrecy, realistically motivated yet also redolent of an escape back to the womb, and their 'sacralisation' in the religious act of sex, which links the 'continuity' of death, loss of self, with a gesture of renewal, procreation, faith in the future. The paradox of the 'secret places' (i.e. Lawrence wants them *not* to remain secret any longer, yet simultaneously reaffirms the privacy and sanctity of the act), springs precisely from hatred of 'social' morality such as Mrs Bolton relays from Tevershall gossip, a morality which is at once puritanical and prurient (like most of the 'popular' discussion of sex in England still, and even some which passes as 'progressive'). Connie and Mellors act out the tragedy of Lawrence's England, which is a tragedy of the bedroom as much as of class divisions, class domination, and industrial ugliness. But it is a tragedy in which no one dies, and in which (hopefully) grace descends without anguish: that is why it is a 'kick against misery'. If it is Christian, which, in important ways, it clearly is, it turns resolutely against the mortification of the flesh in Christian iconography, telling us that the only king who must die is the mechanical centaur of our Waste Land culture. Some have found an element of violence in the lovemaking;[23] but love and hate are both purged in the cult of Iacchos (and no one, surely, would deny their close relationship in life). In point of fact, tragedy is always violent, death being the greatest violence that any organism can sustain; but Lawrence's modern tragedy goes back to the Dionysiac sources of tragic experience for his model of catharsis, or purgation, in which the World Will expresses itself through the 'spirit of music', if we have ears to hear it.

Lady Chatterley's Lover, then, bears witness to Lawrence's large claims for the novel, and its extraordinary ability to assimilate disparate elements. The modes of nineteenth-century realism, romance, tragedy, and perhaps pastoral too, all have some kind of place within the boundaries of this 'novel'.[24] This is one reason why, despite Lawrence's moral intensity, anyone who tried to live by it or up to it would soon find themselves out of their depth. It accomplishes its tragic catharsis on our behalf, but will not allow us, any more than Lawrence's other novels, to 'nail anything down'. This is not to deny its polemical dimension, which encompasses more than a challenging sexual thesis: for this is also a novel about the possibilities that exist for contemporary writing, and how it can overcome its intrinsic processes of alienation. Duncan Forbes, for example, is a very Lawrencian instance of the sick 'modern' artist, a man out of the Loerke stable, and a comparable representative of the radical moral confusion that Lawrence considers to be prevalent (i.e. he cultivates an abstract 'high' art only because he has no capacity for touch, no feeling for the sacral dimension of others, or of the world). At the same time there is a direct and immediate 'shedding of a sickness' in Lawrence's novel, in that the themes he has run together with such insight are drawn immediately from the difficulties of his marriage and his personal situation in life. Every married couple has fantasies of beginning again and recapturing a youthful intensity of desire. Some do it by marrying other partners, while 'adultery' has certainly given many marriages a new lease of life (cf. Malinowski). But Lawrence, as we have seen, opts to give us two very different angles on a relationship simultaneously, and it does look a bit like having your cake and eating it. It is hard to believe that he thought he was describing marriage as it is, or could ever be, for the great majority of people.

Conclusion

This short study has been concerned with Lawrence as a novelist. From time to time critics have emphasised other dimensions of his work; it has been suggested, for example, that his short stories and short novels are better than his full-length works of fiction, because they are more coherent and consistent.[1] Any serious study of free verse would have to give proper attention to Lawrence's poetry. Claims have been made for the literary criticism, and for the paintings, and there is no denying the distinction of both. But in the last analysis Leavis was right (if partly for the wrong reasons) to call his study *D. H. Lawrence: Novelist*, with the insistence in the title that the long works of fiction were more significant than any other part of his *oeuvre*. This is not to belittle the short stories and the novellas; indeed, a writer could have made a reputation from these alone, though it is arguable how much new ground they break in terms of the genres as such. Lawrence's verse, fascinating as it is, makes most sense studied in relation to his prose, and as part of the spiritual autobiography that Lawrence never ceased writing, and which places him, as Leavis observed, in a tradition going back to Bunyan. As a painter, Lawrence has verve and some inspired moments, but is very clumsy. His own description of his 'intuitive' approach to a canvas pretty well sums up the strengths and weaknesses of his method.[2] Intuition is, of course, an important Lawrence trait, and a major value in his imaginative world, but those who see him as a prophet of irrationalism do him a disservice. When he said that he believed in the blood as wiser than the intellect, he was making a point about wisdom as well as a point about blood. It is the novels that engage most profoundly with the imaginative encounter with wisdom, exploring it in a form in which it can be made available to our time.

Obviously this is not such a simple proposition as I have made it sound. There is plenty of room for disagreement about what constitutes wisdom, or experience, and those who dislike the evangelical streak in Lawrence's writings will not easily accept the value of what he has to tell us. For one thing, his own rather cocksure conviction that he had made a major contribution to the women's movement[3] is unlikely to impress; but what I have written may help at any rate to dispel some prejudices about his treatment of gender. *The Rainbow* tells us unequivocally that the evolutionary 'edge' of modern consciousness resides in the female. If history does indeed bear witness to a draining away of 'meaning' as a fixed relation of signifier to signified, it releases, precisely by virtue of this, the whole field of signification for intuition to play over (like the diverse and eclectic cultural fragments of *Women in Love*). The collapse of the patriarchal nineteenth-century consensus, with its rationality and dogmatism, on the battlefields of the First World War, is what makes possible the semantic playfield of *The Lost Girl*, *Mr Noon*, and the three 'political' novels. It is also the *sine qua non* of *Lady Chatterley's Lover*, though there is evidently more than one way of reading Connie's release from the tyranny of the mechanical centaur.

Of course there are very marked limits to Lawrence's radicalism. His profound capacity for empathy with the world, and his inclination to follow the 'flow and recoil' of his own feelings, are reflected in his urge always to place individual relationships at the centre of his fictional world, and to make them the mainstay of his *Lebensphilosophie*. Marriage, for instance, is a crucial concept, even when it is disguised as something else (e.g. extramarital relations). No one could accuse him of not taking sex seriously; but he has been legitimately criticised for representing only a smallish range of possible sexual relations, and doing this so prescriptively that while his own (sometimes idiosyncratic) preferences get a full airing, other people's are relegated to the margins, or actually seen as unacceptable. His commitment to the here and now ('living fully on the spot where you are', which in fact is impossible) can become a sort of anti-intellectual flat-earthing: if he has not actually 'proved it upon the pulses', in Keats's phrase, it does not exist, or exists in the destructive form of a bloodless category (and since most of 'our' civilisation consists of bloodless categories, paranoia inevitably follows).

Politically, it is only too easy to 'deconstruct' Lawrence, but his cultural impact has been much larger than the handful of – largely borrowed – doctrines might suggest. This has something to do with the energy and conviction of his writing; it can also be attributed to the malpractice, established long ago but perpetuated, unfortunately, in feminist readings, of assuming that views expressed by particular characters on particular occasions are definitively the author's own (cf. the description of Tevershall quoted above from *Lady Chatterley's Lover*): to do this is to turn Lawrence into a profoundly self-contradictory writer, of course, but a certain kind of Lawrencian is unperturbed by this. In this way, fragments of Nietzsche, Schopenhauer, Morris, Carlyle, Ruskin, Carpenter and others, woven for good reasons into Lawrence's narrative, were unwoven for less good reasons by his admirers and transformed into a social theory (that of the 'organic community') which at best must be obsolete and naive, and at worst (i.e. if one could imagine it implemented) downright reactionary. Here again we must simply invoke Lawrence's own dictum, which could be an evasion but is not: 'never trust the artist, trust the tale'. Lawrence wants to change his readers' views and attitudes; he does not want to change society. His Utopian politics, indeed, have little use for such a concept as 'society', which is tainted by pragmatism. All his political scenarios have a theatrical air, but they have been interpreted by some people as proto-Fascist because of their uncanny resemblance to almost equally theatrical events in the 'real' world. Evidently, Lawrence is more interested in right-wing solutions to international political and economic problems than in left-wing solutions; but the Soviet Union, which briefly attracted him, had already become a tyranny in his lifetime, and backtracked on many of the Revolution's innovations, while Mussolini's right-wing alternative was still emergent (Lawrence, it should be said, detested what he saw of it). In point of fact Lawrence's novels pronounce a plague on both houses; politics does not have the answer to civilisation's ills. This must be sought in a new conjunction of man and woman, a matter of 'joint work'.[4]

And it is precisely because Lawrence's 'doctrine' takes forms that are close to everyday experience, to the conflicts between men and women as well as their capacity for love and their shared responsibility for the future, in the form of children as well as the planet, that he is still read. Eliot, in response to the proposition that we do not need the writers of the past because we know so much more than they did, replied that 'they are what we know'.[5] Lawrence is one of those writers of the past that (whether we like it or not) we 'know'.

Notes

INTRODUCTION

1. F. R. Leavis's study *D. H. Lawrence: Novelist* (London: Chatto and Windus, 1955) was one of the first books on the author to cut through the biographical myth-making and assess Lawrence as a writer. As such, it is of lasting significance. Leavis followed it with a second book (*Thought, Words, and Creativity: Art and Thought in Lawrence* (London: Chatto and Windus, 1976). Leavis, however, did much more than simply 'revalue' Lawrence, who became for him the cornerstone of a populist ideology dedicated to healing the psychic wounds of post-industrial society. Lawrence's extraordinary sensitivity to the dynamics of community and relationships provided Leavis with a Bible of what he called 'essential English history'. It was left for subsequent commentators (especially Colin Clarke, in *River of Dissolution*, London: Routledge, 1969) to explore the perverse and nihilistic sides of Lawrence, with special reference to the English Romantic tradition.

2. Charles Baudelaire, *Salon of 1846* (Phaidon, 1965). I take Baudelaire, and the critic Walter Benjamin who wrote the definitive study of him, *Charles Baudelaire, a Lyric Poet in the Era of High Capitalism* (NLB, 1976), as touchstones of literary Modernism. Lawrence seems to have known Baudelaire's *Les Fleurs du Mal* (1857–68) well, and to have made telling use of it.

3. D. H. Lawrence, 'Morality and the Novel', in *Phoenix I*, ed. Macdonald (London: Heinemann, 1936).

4. Ibid.

5. Kate Millett, *Sexual Politics* (Hart-Davis, 1970). Millett, in common with many female commentators, finds Lawrence's sexual politics offensive. However, she is not only reluctant to give him the credit he deserves for engaging with the oscillations of love and hate in any normal relationship, she also makes points by misreading and misrepresentation (in her account of the 'Mino' chapter of *Women in Love*, for instance, she objects to Birkin's rhetoric but by selective quotation fails to show that Lawrence does, too).

6. Sheila MacLeod, *Lawrence's Men and Women* (Paladin, 1985). Note also Anne Devlin's recent BBC playscript for *The Rainbow*, in which Ursula's predicament is given a sympathetic Feminist reading.

1 LIFE AND WORKS

1. Harry T. Moore cites the witty poem 'Red Herring' in his definitive

biography of the writer, *Priest of Love* (Heinemann, 1974). The saying seems to have passed out of use somewhat, but an unclassifiable phenomenon/subject/person was referred to as 'neither fish nor flesh nor good red herring'. In this poem, Lawrence describes himself and his brothers and sisters as 'little in-betweens' because they spoke dialect and standard English and had dual class allegiances. The theme of 'in-betweenness' continued to fascinate Lawrence up to the time he wrote *Lady Chatterley's Lover*, where Mellors has a dual personality and speaks two 'languages'.

2. I borrow the title, and something of the substance, of Otto Rank's *The Myth of the Birth of the Hero* (New York: Knopf, 1952). Cf. also *Art and Artist: creative urge and personality development* (New York: Knopf, 1932).

3. Cf. Maurice Beebe, *Sacred Founts and Ivory Towers* (New York University Press, 1964).

4. The cutting of William's hair links him with Samson, and suggests a 'mythic' foreshadowing of his death, as if to make way for Paul.

5. Jessie Weston, *From Ritual to Romance* (New York: Doubleday, 1963).

6. Miriam is never really given a voice in Lawrence's novel. The work in question was the tale entitled 'A Prelude to a Happy Christmas' (*Nottinghamshire Guardian*, 7 December 1907).

7. There seems little point in rehearsing these arguments, though it may be worth pointing out that Lawrence disliked the early Freudian analysis of *Sons and Lovers* (see E. W. Tedlock, *D. H. Lawrence's Sons and Lovers: Sources and Commentary*) (London: University of London Press, 1966).

8. Alice Dax, the prototype of Clara, has given an amusingly off-hand account of her seduction of the young writer (cf. Harry T. Moore, op. cit.)

9. Keith Sagar, among others, has noted how often Lawrence uses the Sleeping Beauty motif, particularly in his later stories, where it seems to embody a much needed compensatory fantasy (though there is often an ironic note).

10. Lawrence mocks these in *Mr Noon*, but in an essay entitled 'Crucifix across the Mountains' (*Twilight in Italy*) he uses them with great imagination to chart a kind of 'stages of the cross' between one culture and another.

11. Lawrence enters into complex relationships with Christ: in some moods, he saw himself as Christ resurrected; in others, he objected to the repressiveness of Christianity.

12. Leavis distorts this argument somewhat, I feel, by restating it in terms of Arnold's opposition of Culture and Anarchy.

13. D. H. Lawrence, *Studies in Classic American Literature*, Introduction.

14. It is interesting to compare C. S. Pierce's semiology of icon, index, sign with the schema in Lawrence's novel whereby the rainbow of 'law' gives way by stages to Ursula's personal vision, with its shifting modalities.

15. Frank Kermode, *D. H. Lawrence* (London: Fontana, 1973).

16. C. Keith Aldritt, *The Visual Imagination of D. H. Lawrence* (London: Edward Arnold, 1971).

17. D. H. Lawrence, *Letters*, Vol. 2, ed. Zytaruk and Boulton (Cambridge University Press, 1981), Letter 732.

18. The name comes from a Hebrew chant that his friend S. S. Koteliansky used to intone.

19. D. H. Lawrence, *Letters*, op. cit., Letter 1104.

20. Cf. G. M. Hyde, *D. H. Lawrence and the Art of Translation* (London: Macmillan, 1980).

21. The terms form the nub of Lawrence's arguments in his *Study of Thomas Hardy*. Frank Kermode explores them in his short study of Lawrence.

22. Lawrence was for a while impressed by developments in the Soviet Union: but of course the abolition of the family there was one of the most disastrous revolutionary policies.

23. Harry T. Moore notes the similarity of the Quetzalcoatl chants to the hymns Lawrence heard as a boy (*The Priest of Love*).

24. D. H. Lawrence, *Etruscan Places* (London: Secker, 1932). Even here, one sees the fascination with 'doing different': Etruria is constructed as an 'alternative' society, by comparison both with Roman civilisation and with modern European.

2 THE ARTIST AS A YOUNG MAN

1. Like Joyce and many of the great Modernists, Lawrence thought of writing as a religious vocation. This sacred/secular ambition was explicit in the poetics of Symbolism, which Arthur Symons rightly saw as religious in inspiration.

2. D. H. Lawrence, *Letters*, Vol. 2, ed. Zytaruk and Boulton (Cambridge University Press, 1981), Letter 667.

3. Frieda seems to have supplied a sort of retrospective conceptual apparatus from her personal experience of psychoanalysis, though Lawrence resented attempts to reduce his novel to a case history.

4. The influence of Frazer's *Golden Bough* (published in 1922) on Lawrence was considerable, as it was on Eliot. Frazer's book was the most compendious of many compilations of myths and legends, and analyses of them, current at the turn of the century and, like the Symbolist movement, formed part of the modern 'search for a soul' and validation of the truth value of literature.

5. Cf. Frank Kermode, op. cit., who finds a 'euphemistically' described 'castration cult' in *The Trespasser*.

6. D. H. Lawrence, *The White Peacock* (Cambridge University Press, 1985), Chapter 6.

7. The Leavisian version of this reworking of the doctrine of the Fall is the idea of the 'organic community', a compendium of Romantic motifs and mythologies which engage only in the most tangential way with reality. This said, there is no doubt that Lawrence was extraordinarily sensitive to 'variations' in cultural patterns, from the mines of Eastwood to the tomb paintings of the Etruscans, and it would be foolish to deny that white Protestant civilisation has impoverished experience even while making enormous strides in science, etc.

8. Frank Kermode, op. cit.
9. Friedrich Nietzsche, *The Birth of Tragedy* (New York: Doubleday, 1962).
10. Ibid.
11. W. B. Yeats, cited in the Penguin *The Trial of Lady Chatterley* (ed. C. H. Rolph, 1961).
12. George Steiner, *The Death of Tragedy* (London: Faber, 1962).
13. Francis Fergusson *The Idea of a Theater* (New York: Doubleday, 1958).
14. Francis Fergusson, op. cit.
15. Otto Rank, op. cit.
16. Jessie Chambers, *D. H. Lawrence: A Personal Record*, by 'E. T.' (London: Cape, 1935).
17. Charles Baudelaire, *L'Héautontimoroumenos* in *Les Fleurs du Mal*.
18. D. H. Lawrence, *Sons and Lovers* (Cambridge University Press, 1987).

3 'ESSENTIAL ENGLISH HISTORY'?

1. Walter Benjamin, 'On some motifs in Baudelaire', in *Illuminations* (London: Fontana, 1968).
2. Cf. Tim Marshall, 'Dialogic Structure', in Roger Fowler, ed., *A Dictionary of Modern Critical Terms* (London: Routledge, 1987).
3. Frank Kermode, op cit.
4. Michael Polanyi, *Personal Knowledge* (London: Routledge, 1958).
5. This, said Lawrence, was what one writes for (for want of a better term), and not for particular groups or individuals. It should be said at once that if Lawrence *did* attach some further significance to the notion of 'race', it was certainly not in the sense of there being any 'master race', still less that this might be WASP.
6. D. H. Lawrence, *Letters*, Vol. 2, ed. Zytaruk and Boulton (Cambridge University Press, 1981), Letter 732.
7. Arthur Rimbaud, letter to Demeny, 15 May 1871.
8. Franz Kafka, *passim*, but especially the 'Letters to Milena', 'Metamorphosis', and 'In the Penal Settlement'.
9. Erich Auerbach, *Mimesis* (Princeton University Press, 1953).
10. D. H. Lawrence, *The Rainbow* (Cambridge University Press, 1985), Chapter 1.
11. Ibid.
12. Ibid., Chapter 2.
13. Ibid., Chapter 6.
14. Ibid., Chapter 7.
15. Ibid., Chapter 8.
16. Aldous Huxley's novel *Point Counter Point* (1928) is one among many instances of the 'musicalisation' of fiction by means of cross-cutting different temporal orders. Joyce uses many such devices in *Ulysses*.
17. D. H. Lawrence, *The Rainbow*, Chapter 11.

18. Ibid., Chapter 10.

19. Matthew Arnold, *Culture and Anarchy* (1869). It is no exaggeration to describe this as one of the key books of contemporary culture, since it formed (via F. R. Leavis, who was deeply influenced by it) the sensibility of more than a generation of English teachers, who found in it a rationale for their subject. Lawrence's work was assimilated to this 'tradition', but only by virtue of excluding some crucial dimensions of it. It was by this route that he became the prophet of the grammar schools.

20. D. H. Lawrence, *The Rainbow*, Chapter 16.

21. W. B. Yeats, 'The Second Coming' in *The Tower* (1918).

22. Letter 732, op. cit.

23. Virginia Woolf, 'Modern Fiction' in *The Common Reader*, Vol. 2.

24. Jane Rye, *Futurism* (London: Studio Vista/Dutton, 1972) remains an excellent introduction to the subject.

25. Roger Sale, 'The narrative technique of *The Rainbow*' in *The Rainbow and Women in Love*. Casebook Series, ed. Colin Clarke, (London: Macmillan, 1969).

26. Ibid.

27. Ibid.

28. D. H. Lawrence, Foreword to *Women in Love* in *Phoenix 2*.

29. D. H. Lawrence, *The Rainbow*, Chapter 6.

30. Ibid.

31. Sale, ibid.

32. *The Rainbow*, Chapter 15.

33. D. H. Lawrence, *Phoenix 1*.

34. Mikhail Bakhtin, *The Dialogic Principle* (University of Texas, 1981). Like Lawrence, Bakhtin has an almost religious belief in the power of the novel to articulate the unseen and to recover the lost totality of experience.

4 'THE EFFECTS OF THE WAR'

1. Stephane Mallarmé, 'Un coup de dés jamais n'abolira le hasard'. One of the seminal texts of literary Modernism, Mallarmé's great poem engages with the play of indeterminacy in the literary work and the ways in which 'meaning' is constituted by association, juxtaposition, and reader/writer relations: in other words by the play of the signifiers. His term 'constellation' is a way of describing the literary text in its open nexus of relations, rather than as a fixed entity.

2. Those who find Lawrence's imagery in this novel violent might do well to consider what barbarism, as well as violations of individual rights and freedoms, were taking place at the Front and (in Lawrence's own 'nightmare' experience) at home.

3. T. S. Eliot, 'The Waste Land', 1922. Eliot's fractured epic is a record of breakdown, his own as well as that of the 'mind' of Europe – which he constituted in his own mind in 'Tradition and the Individual Talent' but which is also embodied in the totalising ideologies of the nineteenth century, severely threatened by the First World War.

4. Alfred, Lord Tennyson's poem 'The Kraken', for all its quaintness, is an interesting precursor of Freud, and a revealing image of Victorianism's hidden depths (fear and repression).

5. D. H. Lawrence, *Women in Love*, Chapter 1.

6. Gudrun's Bloomsbury style of dress, nicely underlined in Ken Russell's film, seems to have riled the Puritan in Lawrence; perhaps for good reasons he could not see Bloomsbury as the answer to the plight of contemporary culture.

7. D. H. Lawrence, *Women in Love*, Chapter 10.

8. Wilhelm Worringer, *Abstraction and Empathy* (1907), a text which became a manifesto of Modernism. After its publication in England (1918) it seemed to express the mood of nihilism of the wartime experience. Its thesis about how 'abstraction' works by using a kind of violence to protect humanity against another, greater, violence has important elements in common with Lawrence's novel.

9. Cf. Colin Clarke, *River of Dissolution* (London: Routledge, 1968).

10. Eliot planned to cut this, the pivotal section of 'The Waste Land', but Pound fortunately dissuaded him.

11. D. H. Lawrence, *Women in Love*, Chapter 8.

12. Ibid., Chapter 19.

13. Ibid., Chapter 20.

14. Ibid.

15. It is the almost incidental allusions like this one that make us realise the extent of Lawrence's Biblical culture.

16. E. M. Forster, *Howard's End* (1910) is a classic 'Edwardian' statement of bad conscience about class. It is bracketed traditionally with the 'condition of England' novels going back to the mid-nineteenth century, and Disraeli's perception that there are 'two nations'; but Forster takes a much more gentle and optimistic view than Lawrence of the traumas and fissures in the English mind.

17. Matthew Arnold, *Culture and Anarchy* (see above, Chapter 3, Note 19).

18. D. M. Mirsky, *The Intelligentsia of Great Britain* (London: Gollancz, 1935).

19. D. H. Lawrence, *Women in Love*, Chapter 8.

20. D. H. Lawrence, 'Introduction to these paintings' in *Phoenix 1*, ed. Macdonald (London: Heinemann, 1936).

21. Ibid.

22. I take this term from Boris Uspensky's still rather neglected *A Poetics of Composition* (University of California, 1973).

23. A reproduction is available in the *Pelican History of Art: Painting and Sculpture in Europe 1880–1940* by G. H. Hamilton (England: Penguin, 1967).

24. D. H. Lawrence, *Women in Love*, Chapter 19.

5 CARNIVALISING THE MIDLANDS

1. Cf. John Worthen, Introduction to *The Lost Girl* (Cambridge University Press, 1981).

2. Ibid.
3. Ibid.
4. Cf. Tedlock, op. cit.
5. D. H. Lawrence, *Letters*, Vol. 2, ed. Zytaruk and Boulton (Cambridge University Press, 1981), Letter 504.
6. Henry James, 'The New Novel' (1914), in *Selected Literary Criticism*, ed. Shapira (London: Heinemann, 1963).
7. Ibid.
8. If Bennett's world has any kind of tragic dimension, it resides very largely in the fact that he seems to recognise at times that the cash values that fascinate him so much rest upon pure convention.
9. Cf. Oswald Ducrot and Tzvetan Todorov, *Dictionnaire encyclopédique des sciences du langage* (Paris: Seuil, 1972).
10. The term *skaz* is widely used in Russian literary theory, where it refers to the survival, and reactivation, of spoken ('oral') narrative modes in a literary text. Gogol, a Ukrainian, was especially alert to the narrative potential of a kind of sub-literary argot, sometimes combined with specific folk elements, and his intricate effects of 'gestural' (highly dramatised and self-dramatising) narrative are based upon the games the narrator can play with his readers and his subject-matter. Hyperbolical rhetorical flourishes strain at the syntax, but turn without warning into self-conscious or uneducated 'mutterings', with a dash of preciosity. Cf. Victor Erlich, *Russian Formalism* (The Hague: Mouton, 1969).
11. D. H. Lawrence, *The Lost Girl*, Chapter 1.
12. Ibid., Chapter 9.
13. Cf. my own study of Lawrence as a translator, *D. H. Lawrence and the Art of Translation* (London: Macmillan, 1981).
14. Arnold Bennett, *The Old Wives' Tale*, Book 3, Chapter 6.
15. D. H. Lawrence, *The Lost Girl*, Chapter 5.
16. Ibid., Chapter 6.
17. John Worthen, op. cit.
18. T. S. Eliot, *Selected Essays* (London: Faber, 1958).
19. D. H. Lawrence, *Letters*, Vol. 3, Letter 2157. Here he describes *Mr Noon* as 'most dangerous'.
20. Cf. Preface to the Cambridge edition.
21. D. H. Lawrence, *Mr Noon*, Chapter 13.
22. Ibid.
23. Mikhail Bakhtin's theory of carnival has made a notable impact upon an age which (as far as England is concerned, at least) is becoming more authoritarian and more anxiously Puritanical. English academics have on the whole interpreted Bakhtin's work in a Marxist way, laying special emphasis on the sociolinguistic components of the dialogic principle, and from one angle Bakhtin's study of Rabelais, with its emphasis on transcoding, transgression, scrambling of codes, up-ending of hierarchies, profanation and sacrilege etc. lends itself to this reading. We should remember, however, that Bakhtin's book was a veiled critique of Stalinism and a fundamentally religious statement of the autonomy of the individual; also that he tried to 'replace' the Marxist concept of 'the people' by a truer and more human populism. It is in this area that his work chimes in

with that of Lawrence; also in his advocacy of 'fictionality' as truer than the ruling ideologies.

24. D. H. Lawrence, *Mr Noon*, Chapter 4.

25. Ibid.

6 LIVING AND PARTLY LIVING

1. There is some similarity to the case of Birkin and Gerald, where the duality is both the Apollo/Dionysus split and the *Doppelgänger* motif. We are also dealing, however, with the 'condition of England' question again, and Forster's anxiety about how to connect the poetry and the prose. As I have suggested, Lawrence's novels cut deeper in more radical ways than Forster's. On the other hand Forster's work is free of Lawrence's bitterness.

2. Cf. my note on *skaz* (Note 10 to Chapter 5), and Viktor Shklovsky's essay 'Art as Technique' in Lemon and Reis, ed., *Four Formalist Essays* (University of Nebraska/Bison Books, 1964).

3. In point of fact the single work from modern fiction that most closely resembles Lawrence's is Doris Lessing's *The Golden Notebook*.

4. This is Lévi-Strauss's term, used to describe a process in both myth and art where elements are freely assembled according to a sort of collage method. The 'bricoleur' is an expert improviser.

5. D. H. Lawrence, *Aaron's Rod*, Chapter 12.

6. Ibid., Chapter 16.

7. *Phoenix 1*, ed. Macdonald (London: Heinemann, 1930).

8. The whole of Chapter 18 ('The Marchesa') is a remarkably subtle account of a liaison that is bound to fail. This chapter alone ought to counteract the view that Lawrence takes a simplistic view of the 'redemptive' power of sexual love; or, indeed, that there is any 'male mystery' being promoted in these late novels that is not undercut by the tale itself.

9. Ibid.

10. D. H. Lawrence, *Letters*, op cit., Letter 2548.

11. D. H. Lawrence, *Kangaroo*, Chapter 1.

12. Ibid., Chapter 10.

13. Cf. Gerard Genette, *Narrative Discourse* (Iowa: Cornell, 1980) and the use made of this term by Roger Fowler, in an essay shortly to be published entitled 'The Lost Girl: Discourse and Focalisation'. The issue of Lawrence's work, since it is in this area that confusions arise about the apparently 'authoritarian' stance of Lawrence's narrator and the seemingly rather arbitrary 'judgmental' positions (often inconsistent) adopted by the narrator/author. Not all critics of Lawrence are responsive to this high degree of narrative mobility.

14. D. H. Lawrence, *Kangaroo*, Chapter 15. This extended autobiographical piece is one of the most important testimonies to Lawrence's experiences during the war, and helps to explain the frequent subsequent references to it in his work.

15. Ibid., Chapter 9. Here again, the 'male power' philosophy attri-

buted to the middle period novels is seen to be a very equivocal phenomenon, and not by any means a simple assertion of 'phallic' domination.

16. I am referring to the Brecht-Lukács debate and other seminal Marxist texts reprinted in *Aesthetics and Politics*, ed. Taylor (London: NLB, 1977). The point is that Fascist theory and practice 'aestheticises politics' by dressing up a repressive order in elaborate regalia, while Marxism in both theory and practice politicises aesthetics by deconstructing its 'absolute' categories and restating them in terms of (historically determined) human praxis. Where Lawrence is concerned, totalitarian ideology is undercut by abrasive satire and insistent dialogism, though the Fascist notion of a final 'solution' continues to exercise a powerful appeal.

17. To come down finally on one side or the other (Fascist or Marxist) would be a 'mistake', it seems. Characteristically, Lawrence promotes open-endedness, whatever his protagonists may do.

18. 'Bleak' is right, I think, but here again one is amazed at its power to endure endless vicissitudes.

19. I take this observation from his preface to the Penguin volume of short stories, though other critics have said more or less the same thing. Of course, it should not be overstated, nor is Lawrence systematic about it.

20. I suppose none of us would like to define what an 'individual' is; but I mean that Lawrence maintains a non-conformist stance *vis-à-vis* even the totalising philosophies he makes play with.

21. See my note (Chapter 3, Note 5) on Lawrence and race. It should be said that the racial stereotyping of *The Plumed Serpent* is resented by some Mexicans known to me.

22. Antonin Artaud, *Le Théâtre et son Double* (Paris: Gallimard, 1964). This pioneering work of a rather deranged mind more or less defined the methods of the Theatre of Cruelty and it is relevant that Artaud's Mexican experiences should have influenced his philosophy of the theatre.

7 NAMING THE PARTS

1. Cf. F. R. Leavis, *Anna Karenina and Other Essays* (London: Chatto, 1971). Leavis is concerned to defend Tolstoy's novel against what he sees as an uncharacteristically obtuse attack by Lawrence (in the *Letters* and elsewhere) on Tolstoy the disenchanted sensualist who insists on scoring a moral victory over Anna. It is Lawrence's view that Anna 'belongs' to Vronsky rather than to her dull husband, a view clearly related to the situation of Lawrence and Frieda.

2. In 'Pornography and Obscenity' (*Phoenix 1*) Lawrence tells us that there is 'an element of pornography in nearly all nineteenth-century literature' because 'there is sex excitement with a desire to spite the sexual feeling, to humiliate it, and degrade it, and as soon as this happens the element of pornography enters'. He cites the 'slightly indecent titillations' of *Jane Eyre*, *The Mill on the Floss*, and *Anna Karenina*. This position corresponds quite closely to that of many feminists, except that Lawrence does not specify that it is women who are 'humiliated' and 'degraded'.

3. Jessie L. Watson, *From Ritual to Romance* is a product of the very literary Cambridge school of anthropology, and it had a considerable influence on many writers, most notably Eliot. Quite apart from such influences, Jessie Weston's undertaking in providing a mythic rationale for literature was symptomatic of a contemporary anxiety, one that Lawrence shared.

4. Frank Harris, *My Life and Loves*, ed. John F. Gallagher (W. H. Allen, 1964).

5. I use the Wagnerian term consciously. Lawrence's great romance develops a smallish number of extraordinarily rich themes through an elaborate texture of 'chromatic' sequences; its relation to any 'real' world is evidently problematic.

6. It seems to me that this kind of relationship, or a relevant recognition of its absence, must form part of a definition of erotic literature as opposed to pornography, where relationships, such as they are, are purely functional.

7. A return to England and to the genre of the 'condition of England' novel, for one thing; but also to the early preoccupation with the 'idyll' and in a sense to the themes of *Sons and Lovers*, where 'Mellors' combines two 'Morels', father and son, perhaps resolving Lawrence's life-long Oedipal problem. The Golden Bough-ish landscape is also a kind of regression.

8. From Dorothy Brett's account, Lawrence suffered from impotence; this probably accounts for the immoderate fear of Bertha's sexuality articulated by Mellors.

9. This picks up the preoccupation with 'bits' in (for example) *Kangaroo*.

10. Language and class, primarily, but the 'code-switching' has a symbolic role as well in defining the 'outsider'.

11. Cf. Bronislaw Malinowski, *Sex, Culture and Myth* (London: Hart-Davis, 1967).

12. Ibid. The findings are idiosyncratic, but well documented.

13. D. H. Lawrence, *Lady Chatterley's Lover*, Chapter 4.

14. W. B. Yeats, quoted (the Fifth Day) in *The Trial of Lady Chatterley* (Penguin, 1961).

15. It is a gentle affirmation of the need for continuity, but it links them both with Sir Clifford, too, and the question of an heir.

16. The film had atmosphere and sometimes the right 'tonality', but was inevitably a vehicle for Sylvia Kristel, who, though sometimes poignant, lacked the emotional range for the part.

17. Cf. *Women in Love*. Colin Clarke's study of Lawrence, *River of Dissolution* (London: Routledge, 1968), remains indispensable.

18. Cf. Leavis's treatment of this theme (op. cit.).

19. D. H. Lawrence, *Lady Chatterley's Lover*, Chapter 11.

20. See Chapter 5, Note 5. This is why modern tragedy is a kind of contradiction in terms (cf. the *Study of Thomas Hardy* and Introduction to Verga's *Cavalleria Rusticana*).

21. The influence of Nietzsche persists throughout Lawrence's work, far beyond *The Trespasser*, and it grows in intensity and profundity. *Lady Chatterley's Lover*, for example, is consistent with the arguments of Nietz-

sche's *The Birth of Tragedy*, especially with regard to the fragile 'principle of individuation' that shapes the self.

22. Morris's *News from Nowhere* (1891) and other Utopian Socialist works left their mark on Lawrence, bringing together aestheticism and socialism.

23. Feminists rightly object to the mainly passive part played by Connie throughout; but an episode like that in which Mellors abruptly 'takes' her, out of doors, does not seem to me inapposite in context. It seems to me perverse to deny the presence of elements of the chase in sexual relations.

24. Many elements in the book relate directly to the process of writing, from Sir Clifford's literary ambitions to Lawrence's passionate disquisitions upon the uses of fiction. There is also a rudimentary critique of language, and I have tried to suggest the presence of operatic and balletic, rather than realistic, elements.

CONCLUSION

1. It was partly to challenge this view that Leavis wrote his book, with some success.

2. 'Introduction to these Paintings', in *Phoenix 1*. The paintings are not simply naive, of course; there is a polemical engagement going on with the other kinds of post-impressionism, especially as represented by Bloomsbury.

3. This was said specifically in relation to *The Lost Girl*, but there is no doubt that Lawrence on the one hand experienced life from a woman's standpoint, and on the other had absolutely no conception of what needed to be fought for, or how to go about it.

4. At all events, Lawrence felt this way in the early days of his married life. If things changed a bit later on, he never altogether lost sight of this precept.

5. This is a conservative philosophy of culture, of course; but we ought to bear in mind Eliot's propositions about the present influencing the past (*Tradition and the Individual Talent*).

Select Bibliography

I have worked as far as possible from the Cambridge University Press Edition of Lawrence's novels, under the general editorship of James T. Boulton and Warren Roberts. Where Cambridge editions have not been available, I have used Penguin texts. Other major references are as follows:

Aldritt, Keith, *The Visual Imagination of D. H. Lawrence* (London: Edward Arnold, 1971).

Arnold, Matthew, *Culture and Anarchy* (London: Smith, Elder, 1869).

Artaud, Antonin, *Le Théâtre et son Double* (London: John Calder, 1964).

Auerbach, Erich, *Mimesis* (Princeton: Princeton University Press, 1953).

Bakhtin, Mikhail, *The Dialogic Principle* (Texas: University of Texas, 1981).

Bakhtin, Mikhail, *Rabelais and his World* (Boston: M.I.T., 1968).

Baudelaire, Charles, *Salon of 1846* (London: Phaidon, 1965).

Baudelaire, Charles, *Les Fleurs du Mal* (Oxford: O.U.P., 1958).

Beebe, Maurice, *Sacred Founts and Ivory Towers* (New York: New York University Press, 1964).

Benjamin, Walter, *Charles Baudelaire, a Lyric Poet in the Era of High Capitalism* (London: New Left Books, 1968).

Benjamin Walter, *Illuminations* (London: Collins, 1968).

Chambers, Jessie, *D. H. Lawrence: A Personal Record*, by 'E. T.' (London: Cape, 1935).

Clarke, Colin, *River of Dissolution* (London: Routledge and Kegan Paul, 1969).

Clarke, Colin, ed. *The Rainbow and Women in Love* (London: Macmillan, 1969).

Ducrot, Oswald and Todorov, Tsvetan, *Dictionnaire encyclopédique des sciences du langage* (Paris: Editions de Seuil, 1972).

Eliot, T. S., 'The Waste Land' (London: Faber and Faber, 1922).

Eliot, T. S., *Collected Essays* (London: Faber and Faber, 1963).

Erlich, Victor, *Russian Formalism* (The Hague: Mouton, 1969).

Fergusson, *The Idea of a Theater* (New York: Doubleday, 1958).

Fowler, Roger, *A Dictionary of Modern Critical Terms* (London: Routledge and Kegan Paul, 1987).

Forster, E. M., *Howard's End* (London: Edward Arnold, 1910).

Frazer, Sir James, *The Golden Bough* (London: Macmillan, 1922).

Genette, Gerard, *Narrative Discourse* (Iowa: University of Iowa, 1980).

Harris, Frank, *My Life and Loves*, ed. Gallaher (London: W. H. Allen, 1964).

Huxley, Aldous, *Point Counter Point*, (London: Chatto and Windus, 1928).

Hyde, G. M., *D. H. Lawrence and the Art of Translation* (London: Macmillan, 1980).

James, Henry, *Selected Literary Criticism*, ed. Shapira (London: Chatto and Windus, 1963).

Lawrence, D. H. *Phoenix 1*, ed. Macdonald (London: Heinemann, 1936).

Leavis, F. R., *D. H. Lawrence: Novelist* (London: Chatto and Windus, 1955).

Leavis, F. R., *Thought, Words and Creativity: Art and Thought in Lawrence* (London: Chatto and Windus, 1976).

Leavis, F. R., *Anna Karenina and Other Essays* (London: Chatto and Windus, 1971).

Lemon and Reis, eds., *Four Formalist Essays* (Nebraska: University of Nebraska, 1964).

Malinowski, Bronislaw, *Sex, Culture, and Myth* (London: Collins, 1967).

Moore, Harry T., *Priest of Love* (London: Penguin, 1974).

Millett, Kate, *Sexual Politics* (London: Virago, 1979).

MacLeod, Sheila, *Lawrence's Men and Women* (London: Macmillan, 1985).

Mirsky, D. M., *The Intelligentsia of Great Britain* (London: Gollancz, 1935).

Nietzsche, Friedrich, *The Birth of Tragedy* (New York: Doubleday, 1962).

Polanyi, Michael, *Personal Knowledge* (London: Routledge and Kegan Paul, 1958).

Rank, Otto, *The Myth of the Birth of the Hero* (New York: Doubleday, 1952).

Rolph, C. H., ed., *The Trial of Lady Chatterley* (London: Penguin, 1961).

Rye, Jane, *Futurism* (London: Studio Vista, 1972).

Steiner, George, *The Death of Tragedy* (London: Faber and Faber, 1962).

Taylor, Ronald, ed., *Aesthetics and Politics* (London: New Left Books, 1977).

Tedlock, E. W., *D. H. Lawrence's Sons and Lovers: Sources and Commentary* (London: Weidenfeld and Nicolson, 1966).

Uspensky, Boris, *A Poetics of Composition* (California: University of California, 1973).

Weston, Jessie, L., *From Ritual to Romance* (New York: Doubleday, 1963).

Worringer, Wilhelm, *Abstraction and Empathy*, (first published in Germany in 1907 as *Abstraktion und Einfuhlung*) (London: Routledge and Kegan Paul, 1968).

Index

131